TEEN vs TARGET

Build extreme confidence, dial-in laser focus,
and fearlessly compete to win in clays,
school and life

BOB PALMER

Author of the MIND vs TARGET Series

WHAT PEOPLE ARE SAYING ABOUT BOB PALMER AND TEEN vs TARGET

ATHLETE SUCCESS STORIES

"I set a goal of winning an Olympic medal and became very good at the sport, but I was lacking in mental skills and my scores showed it. Bob taught me valuable techniques to use on and off the range and helped me get to the next level, which led to a silver medal victory at the Paris 2024 Olympic Games."

— **CONNER PRINCE**, Olympic Silver Medalist Paris 2024 - International Skeet, USA

"Working with Bob completely changed everything for me in the pool. For so long, I thought my setbacks were just physical—bad meets, missed times and off practices—but once I opened up about the mental side, I realized how much was really going on under the surface. Working through that gave me a whole new sense of clarity, confidence, and control. I started swimming with more purpose and less pressure. It didn't just improve my performance—it made me love the sport."

— **SAMMY BAKER**, USA

"Thanks to Bob's training, I was able to reach and stay in my Zone when it mattered most—and it helped me take home a Collegiate National Championship."

— **BRINLEY GOTT**, USA

"Working with my mental performance coach, Bob Palmer, has completely transformed my game. His tools helped me stay focused under pressure and consistently perform at my peak. His guidance has been a game-changer in my journey to the top."

— **LAVANYA GUPTA**, India

"I acquired skills, in my time working with Bob, that helped translate what I was able to do in practice to competition. I gained confidence in my ability to perform when needed. The skills I learned from Bob Palmer extended beyond the shotgun range and into other aspects of life. I was able to perform better in school exams and in my professional experiences. What I learned also helped me with professional interviews and my performance in my professional field."

— **NICK MASSEY**, USA

"Bob's program has taken my sporting clays game to the next level. He has successfully distilled the winning mindset."

— **JONATHAN L. PRINCE**, USA

"Bob Palmer's training - It has been miraculous!"

— **KEVIN GARDENHIRE**, USA

"I started working with Bob Palmer and his high-performance system ten years ago. I was at a "crossroads" in my life and Bob helped me move on from the heavy anchors holding me back. With his help, I chose the path of excellence and it has been quite a ride, with endless learning and lots of practical experience. The rewards? Lots of big victory smiles."

— **JULIAN PEÑA**, Spain

"As a professional golfer, one of the most important aspects of being successful is having a very strong mental game. And before I started working with Bob I always felt lacking in that part of my game. Bob not only gave me the tools to become better as a golfer/sportsman but gave me tools to handle all the problems that life throws at a person. Through Bob I have come to believe that with the right training of your mind one can achieve things that seemed impossible to achieve. I will forever be grateful to him for his help."

— **AMARDEEP (HAMMER) MALIK**, India

"Bob is a listener who directs you to the "Zone." And I've made my performance, lifestyle and leadership better because of that Zone!"

— **SETH INMAN**, USA

"I began working with Bob Palmer as a young skeet shooter around the age of twelve. The mental game learned through Bob Palmer taught me to avoid negative energy and distractions. It has magnified my ability to use my adrenaline rush to shape what I am thinking into positive energy while in the Zone, and has boosted my confidence level, which has created consistency and focus, turning my mental game into a winning mindset."

— **SHEAFFER STANFILL**, USA

"Put your hearing protection in, connect to Bluetooth, and go find the ZONE!"

— **BRAYDEN COSPER**, USA

"I want to express my gratitude for your invaluable coaching and support. Your guidance in focus and adrenaline management has truly made a difference in my performance and mindset."

— **COLLINS PRESCOTT**, USA

PARENT AND COACH SUCCESS STORIES

"When I began to work with Bob to prepare for the world stage in track and field, I didn't realize how much his teachings would extend beyond sport. His methods helped me sharpen my focus and take ownership of my mindset while building the confidence and resilience needed to perform under pressure in any situation. Today, as a coach, I see how essential these tools are for every athlete to have in their repertoire. For any parent, this book offers invaluable lessons that support a fulfilling journey in sport and set in place strong foundations for success in all areas of life."

— **JESSICA ZELINKA**, Heptathlete and Hurdler, Two-Time Olympian, Canadian Champion, Coach and Parent, Canada

"Give your child the boost in their competitive sport by using Bob's program and coaching techniques. Starting my daughter out with a solid mental foundation has already helped her surpass her peers in her sports! Bonus — she applies these mental edge techniques in Gymnastics, Swimming, and Cheer. Give your high performing athlete the edge with this program!"

— **TAYLOR HODGES**, Parent, USA

"He is finally figuring out how to have success while enjoying the process. I can't begin to tell you how much it lowers the stress of competition and his results are improving along with his outlook!"

— **GEORGE WILEY**, Parent, USA

"Working with Bob Palmer has been truly life-changing for our daughter and our entire family. Before we started this journey with Bob, our child was doing well, but struggled emotionally when it came to the pressures of competing at a higher level. Bob created a safe, supportive mental space by giving her tools to build her self-confidence and drown out the background noise.

Over a short period of time, we saw a remarkable transformation — not just in behavior, but in mindset. Our child now approaches challenges with confidence and resilience...The tools and strategies Bob shared have not only helped in the competitive arena, but also in everyday life. We are deeply grateful for the care, insight, and dedication Bob brought to every session with our daughter. He is a master in his craft and we are forever grateful for the care, dedication and insight he brought to every session and phone call with our daughter."

— **MATT AND SHAUNA SITRA**, Parent, USA

"The training that Bob has given to my son, Luke, helped him not only be competitive in his sport but in life skills as well. He was able to utilize his training on the field in shotgun sports, in the classroom and in his approach to everyday life. It is something he will carry with him for life."

— **BRANDI PRIESTLY**, Parent, USA

"Bob's work on "the Zone" has helped my elite and para-karate athletes overcome fear and anxiety, sharpen focus, and perform with confidence at the podium level."

— **SENSEI HEATHER FIDYK**, Head Instructor - South Calgary Karate Club, Canada

"Control over the mental game is the difference between good and great. As a coach, parent, and instructor I searched for a system that teaches the best way to dominate the mental game. The Zone, taught by Bob Palmer, is an indispensable tool for success! He taught and instructed athletes that achieved multiple high school, state, and collegiate championship titles in trap and skeet shooting disciplines."

— **PAUL DIETZ**, Parent and Coach, USA

"Bob, I sincerely appreciate your exceptional support and guidance to Jaivir. My intuition about you was spot on…As a parent, I understand that we try our best, but we sometimes need someone to rely on. You have given Jaivir hope, and your unwavering support has been a great help to his well-being and emotional growth. He feels motivated to do better, and that is all because of you. Your dedication to your role is commendable, and we are incredibly grateful for the profound and positive impact you have had on Jaivir's life. What a remarkable transformation this has been!"

— **YADAVINDER DHILLON**, Parent, India

"[Bob Palmer's] program not only provided our child with a skillset that builds resilience, but taught us as parents our role and how to be of maximum effectiveness and support to our child. The simple truth is, I became a better parent and person because of SportExcel. My son was able to achieve his goal of playing college baseball with a significant scholarship. We do not believe this goal would have been reached without SportExcel. Grades, work performance, leadership, focus, and stability all increased based on principles learned from the SportExcel program. I give the highest recommendation possible to Bob Palmer and the SportExcel program."

— **JASON DAVIS**, Parent, USA

"Bob's vision of the Zone is contagious. Find the ZONE as a coach or a parent coach and your young shooter will EXCEL! Embrace the competitive edge of technology and go break 'em all!"

— **ROBERT COSPER**, Coach/Parent, USA

"We would like to thank you over and over again for your unbelievable talent in bringing athletes back to success. Without you my son wouldn't be as happy and confident as he is today. He is more focused, passionate, dedicated and calm. I am extremely proud of him. Thank you so much again for your help, support, motivation and encouragement."

— **PARENT OF A MINOR**, Canada

"My son is back to a level he belongs to. He accepted an offer from an elite team! Thank you very much for all the tools and strategies you taught him!"

— **PARENT OF A MINOR**, Canada

"We are incredibly grateful for the profound and positive impact you have had on our son's life. What a remarkable transformation this has been!"

— **PARENT OF A MINOR**, India

"Both my son and I, talking to each other from a "Zone" perspective, is amazing. I don't think we have ever communicated as well as we are currently. I am shocked at how immediate the results are. He is opening up constantly, both with his feelings / thoughts, and also with questions! Shooting sports set aside, this is just what the doctor ordered for the relationship we have!"

— **PARENT OF A MINOR**, USA

"Just letting you know, for a moment today I felt a little anxious watching my son compete and immediately recognized it. I used your technique and was immediately calm. I don't know if he recognizes it, but it's helped his confidence in his sport tremendously! Many thanks, Bob."

— **PARENT OF A MINOR**, USA

WHAT TEEN ATHLETE REVIEWERS HAVE TO SAY

"One of my favorite parts of TEEN vs TARGET is the emphasis on academic GPA and performance in the classroom. The teen demographic is generally not as focused on how important a GPA can be when looking for options to do their sport in college. This is something that many athletes can work on to help them better their experience, whether it's at the recruitment stage before college or even during college."

— **TEEN vs TARGET REVIEWER**

"I appreciate that TEEN vs TARGET speaks on the topic of anxiety as many athletes experience this before ever having any success with their team or in a new situation. I also like the competition preparation method that is given. The ZONE is starting to come full circle with how it is used in my clays sport."

— **TEEN vs TARGET REVIEWER**

"I like the idea of using feedback very much. I believe that the feedback exercise in TEEN vs TARGET gives you an easier, more consistent path to victory and could help a lot of athletes and how they handle decision-making with their sport."

— **TEEN vs TARGET REVIEWER**

"I found the emphasis in TEEN vs TARGET on having pre-competition time to focus is super important, and I also like how it emphasizes boundaries for teammates and coaches."

"The impact that this book's lessons for my sport have also had on my grades has been amazing. I believe that the examples Bob gave and the strategies are very helpful to someone that doesn't necessarily know where to start with improving school grades."

TEEN vs TARGET

Copyright © 2025 SportExcel Inc.

ISBN: 978-1-7770623-8-5

Published by SportExcel Inc.

www.sportexcel.ca

bpalmer@sportexcel.ca

DISCLAIMER

The information contained in this book is made available by
SportExcel Inc. It is to be used strictly for educational purposes
only. SportExcel Inc. does not offer any psychological, professional,
medical, financial, personal or legal advice and none of the
information contained in this book should be confused as such
advice. Results of using the SportExcel High-Performance System
may vary from individual to individual.

FOR MY GRANDCHILDREN

Max, Adeline, Maeve, Emma, Daemon, Sam and Mia

PUBLISHER'S NOTE

As clays covers multiple sports from skeet to trap to sporting to FITASC to international versions of each, this book is designed to be applied in all of these sports. A station, post, stand, and pad will all be referred to as the stand.

As well, this book can be used for other sports as the program and program strategies are extremely impactful—all you have to do is substitute your sport name whenever I mention clays or clay targets. That said, keep your eyes peeled for the more generic sports version of this book that will be coming in the future.

TABLE OF CONTENTS

ACKNOWLEDGMENTS

Grateful acknowledgment is made to the following people for their contribution to the writing and creation of this book:

My family for their support throughout this project.

Caron Palmer, business expert, mentor, partner and spouse—for project management, cover design and publishing.

Terry Heeg, media expert and long-time editor and motivator—for editing, professional advice and mentoring.

Leb (Nonon Tech & Design), for his wonderful work in formatting the book.

A special thank you to our teen and young adult reviewers who helped ensure the content resonated with readers:
    JJ Peters, Former NCAA Hockey Player – USA
    Carmen Griffiths, 2024-25 National Golf Squad – Scotland
    DJ Miller, College Student, International Trap Shooter – USA
    Anika Zelinka-Miller, 2025 U16 NCL All-Star Waterpolo Team – Canada
    The Dukart Family, Multi-sport – USA

All of my clients, children and grandchildren who taught me the importance of accepting feedback and improving my game as a trainer, parent and grandfather.

FOREWORD
By Terry Heeg

Dear teen athletes:

Wow! Pull. Bang. Poof!

If you have a copy of this book, get ready for the best rest of your life. As author Bob Palmer says, "I wish I could have had this system when I was young." So, Bob has put this system together for you in a quite easy-to-read format, and you will even have some fun along the way as you navigate how to succeed, how to win and how to be a champion.

I first met Bob 20 years ago when he started writing his column *Own the Zone* for TRAP & FIELD MAGAZINE. After editing just a few of his articles, I said, "Bob, this not only applies to being a champion shooter, this also applies to life!" I later asked Bob to write an additional column specifically directed for the youth shooters in the sport of American trapshooting.

While this book speaks directly to the clay target shooting sports, Bob is a high-performance trainer in many other sports and walks of life. His approach to teaching is *sui generis* (unique/one-of-a-kind) offering easy solutions to overcome obstacles. Yes, he covers the bad stuff, too, like nervousness, having a bad event, dealing with bullies and lots more.

It was an honor to edit this book. It encouraged me and inspired me, and I am quite sure it will do the same for you. So, if you are ready to read TEEN vs TARGET - Then get set and go!

— TERRY HEEG,

Retired Editor-in-Chief - TRAP & FIELD MAGAZINE,

The Official Magazine of the Amateur Trapshooting Association

COACH'S PLAYBOOK
By John Lilly

As you're now holding TEEN vs TARGET in your hands, you're already different—curious enough to want more from your shooting than just being an "okay" shooter.

Shooting clay targets is more than just about improving your scores. It's about discovering what you're made of when the pressure is on, learning to handle setbacks, and finding out just how far you can go when you use your nerves, doubts, and challenges to fuel you to get better. This book helps with all that and more. And not just your shooting game—everything—school and life.

Look, I'm not going to sugarcoat this. The journey you're on isn't always going to feel good. There will be days when you miss targets you know you should have hit. Days when your mind feels like it's working against you instead of with you. Days when you wonder if you're cut out for this sport at all.

But here's what I've learned coaching everyone from nervous beginners to Olympic-level athletes over more than a dozen years: Those uncomfortable moments? They're not roadblocks, they're rocket fuel, as Bob's system will show you how to use them to launch your game into the stratosphere.

This book isn't just another shooting manual. Bob Palmer—the Master—shows you how to get in the ZONE, how to develop real LEADERSHIP skills, and how to achieve the OUTCOMES you're dreaming about. But be warned: his approach only works if you're willing to go all in. There are no half-measures and no shortcuts.

Using Bob's method, I've helped hundreds of young shooters transform their game and who they become as people. The confidence they build on the range carries over into school, relationships, and life decisions. The mental toughness they develop helps them push through all life's challenges that would have stopped them cold before.

Plus, you build relationships in this sport with the strategies Bob teaches you—with teammates, coaches, even competitors—and it will blow you away. Some of my closest friendships started with someone standing next to me in the stand.

TEEN vs TARGET is the book title—but it's also your reality. Every time you call for that target, it's you rising above everything that tries to hold you back—your doubts, your fears and your beliefs limiting you about what you can achieve. But now, with this book in your hands, you're already different, and it's up to you to prove that to yourself.

Welcome to the journey.

— **JOHN LILLY,**
Shooting Coach/Business Executive

INTRODUCTION
FOR PARENTS AND COACHES

Why your teen athlete needs this book

> *Do you know what my favorite part of the game is? The opportunity to play.*
>
> **MIKE SINGLETARY,**
> Star Coach

You're giving your teen athlete every opportunity—equipment, financial backing, coaching and emotional support. You agonize when they melt down, cheer when they succeed, and, quite literally, feel every up and down shift of their emotions. You only want the best for your athlete.

And that is what this book is all about, as giving young athletes the best has been my mission for more than 30 years. I've put my heart, soul and expertise on the line to empower young athletes to succeed. In a very real sense, I also wrote this book for my long-ago athlete self, as I remember my frustration as a young athlete when I had no place to turn for advice.

This book, part of my SportExcel program and the MIND vs TARGET Series, fills that gap. It offers you and your teen the opportunity to take charge of their clays game, their education and their life—with an approach to sport high performance unknown when I was young and still largely lacking in sport to this day. Every word is designed to give your teen confidence, consistency, resilience, empowerment and more fun. I pull out all the stops to empower your teen via strategies for developing leadership—in the stand, in the classroom and in their future career.

I've worked hard to write this book in a manner that will engage teens. I've gleaned all the tools from the feedback I've gotten from three decades of face-to-face interactions with thousands of young athletes, as well as from the teens and young adults who reviewed this book prior to publishing. I've enjoyed the highs when athletes win and and mentored them through their lows—across high school, college, pro and Olympic sports.

This book includes real sport examples from these interactions, plus my extensive experiences as the CEO and high-performance trainer for SportExcel, as a karate sensei and club owner and as a national competitor. I use these stories to demystify high performance and make achieving success normal for your teen—not something extraordinary, but normal.

Over the past 30 years, my MIND vs TARGET program has propelled thousands of teen athletes to success. Their parents and coaches (my fans) have described my program "as giving their athlete a huge advantage" and "being an essential part of their equipment," as they have had ring-side seats and have observed the fast and long-term gains in sport performance. And while the tools greatly impact sport, parents also acknowledge and are blown away by the carryover effect into every aspect of their teen's life, academics and peer-group leadership.

That said, there is usually one thing lacking in most high-performance programs and that is the involvement of you, the parent and/or coach. I'll ask you to do your part and read this book right along with your teen athlete so you'll experience the effectiveness of the tools and be better able to support them in their high-performance journey. You'll create a dynamic family/team high-performance synergy that is the bedrock of all winning athletes.

I believe that you will gain such a profound level of understanding of high performance that, like me, you'll wish you had had this program when you were playing youth sports back in the day!

Enjoy and participate in your teen's high-performance Zone!

Be the Zone,

— BOB PALMER, *CEO,*
SportExcel CEO, High-Performance Trainer, Author and
4th-Degree Karate Sensei

" *Mental will is a muscle that needs exercise,
just like muscles of the body.*

— LYNN JENNINGS,
Star Runner "

TEEN vs TARGET PLAYBOOK

OVERVIEW: UPLOADING WINNING TO YOUR BRAIN

Your brain has an operating system and apps, just like your cell phone. And you are going to use your brain as brilliantly as you use your cell phone, but for winning.

You have in your hands the playbook for tapping into success.

" *The mind controls the body. If you can control*
your mind, you can control your shot.

— MATT EMMON,
Star Olympic Shooter

"

1
THE CHAMPION'S PATHWAY

Learn to win in sport, school and life.

My goal is to turn you into a champion and a high achiever in your sport, your school and your life. We'll be focusing on sport primarily, and I expect that by reading (and rereading) this book (plus loads of practicing), you'll see huge improvements in your game and in other areas of your life as well, partly by driving fearlessly toward your goals, partly by fixing what is currently getting in the way of your success, but mostly by understanding that your brain is as easy to upgrade as your phone—and using that understanding to win.

When I played sports as a teen, a lot of things stopped me. My game was hockey, not clays, and I loved it. And sometimes I played really *well*, and sometimes I played *poorly*, and sometimes I played *just awful*. And sometimes I played *well*, *poorly* and *awful* in the same game.

I hated that inconsistency. I hated the embarrassment and pressure. And I really hated failing at my game, and worrying what others were thinking about me. As I grew older, I could feel my opportunities slipping away as tryouts for teams went poorly and I got cut. None of this fitted into my goal of being a champion.

At age 32, I got a second chance in the sport of karate. Now age 32 may sound really old to you, but this time around I was smarter. And I had a number of other pieces in place—like college degrees in Systems and Education that led me to believe that high performance should be simple. It had to be simple because at times I had played really well, brilliantly even, without even trying. It just seemed to happen.

So, thinking back to how those moments of brilliance in hockey had been so easy, I started asking myself questions. Such as:

- How had I felt no nervousness and no pressure?
- How had mistakes been overcome effortlessly, without thinking?
- How in some games did my skills suddenly get way, way better?
- Where did the euphoria, fun and fearlessness come from?
- And why was it so hard to sustain that level for a whole game and beyond?

The result, a system

In my sport of karate, all of these questions eventually got answered with tournament victories and the huge achievement of earning my 4th-degree black belt. My experiences of playing hockey, coaching and competing in karate and training gold-medal Olympians all came together for this program.

This six-step system for winning took my game and the game of many of my clients to the podium. I have full expectations that it will take your game way beyond where you are now to winning and podium successes as well.

A system is like a formula such as a math equation. It's straightforward and repeatable. You plug in the numbers in a math formula and it gives you a result every time. My main goal is to give you this system so that you can plug in your goals, apply your training and become a champion by creating consistency, focus and resilience. I'll be teaching you a whole new way of thinking about and playing your game. And instead of thinking of it as a math formula, I'll be using the communication system you call a cell phone.

What you'll learn

I think you'll really like this aspect of this book. I've made the process of becoming a champion as easy to undertake as operating your cell phone. As a matter of fact, we are going to use your knowledge of cell phone technology (which is likely huge) and use it to illustrate the system.

You'll see this cell phone image throughout the book. From chapter to

chapter, we'll fill in the blanks, installing a high-performance operating system and a whole array of applications (tools) as we go. It is designed to make learning to win fun, and practically a done deal.

With each new chapter, you'll learn how to upgrade your "mental" operating system, the mindset that powers everything you do. Plus, you'll learn to "install" the habits of champions right into your daily life, just as easy as adding a new app to your phone. This book is packed with simple, app-inspired tactics that help you crush it on the range, ace your classes, and step up in everything you do. Think of each strategy as a new tool on your home screen, just like in the diagram. It's easy to access, always there when you need it, and built to help you win.

But let's be real, as success isn't just a tap away. While you'll have to put in the work, these proven app-like strategies are designed to make your journey smoother. Just like your favorite apps, they're quick to "install," fun to use, and deliver real results. Whether you're aiming for perfect rounds in clays, mastering a tough subject, or just trying to feel more confident in different social situations, you'll find the right "download" for every challenge.

It's now time to swipe your way to your personal best with an overview of the six steps of this system, where you'll discover how this cell-phone-inspired journey through high performance will boost your game, your grades, and your confidence.

Step 1: Ignite your high-performance mind

In Step 1, you'll learn to ignite your system with a power-up button that we'll call the GO-ZONE. You'll love it, as it is like the power-up button on your cell phone that no coach probably has ever told you about.

But it's real. And it will start in the next chapter with you pretending to be an archaeologist so you can dig down into your memories and uncover your greatest and most pleasant sports experiences.

These experiences probably felt electric, fun and exciting. And that is the same way you'll describe your power-up button when you learn it, as it is designed to make every practice and game feel electric, fun and exciting.

Step 2: Supercharge your sport vision

In Step 2, you develop your goals into masterful visions of your future. You are going to deal with nervousness. I'm sure the idea of having no nerves seems remote and for some of you very nervous types quite inconceivable at this point, especially with the current belief being that you have to accept and embrace nerves as a normal part of our game.

Wrong. Get ready for the new reality of a nerves-free game. No longer will you ever fear being nervous at center stage in the big competition. Or nervous for the year-end exam at school. You will learn to create outstanding visions of success that are highly empowered by adrenaline.

These visions will reinforce a new and euphoric way of thinking, feeling and competing. You'll refer to these empowered selfies as VSELFIES, the first part of building a powerful operating system for winning.

Step 3: Navigate the pressures of competition

In Step 3, you'll identify your blocks to success. All the stuff that gets in your way and perhaps makes you feel sad, frustrated or angry, such as:

- Missing easy targets.
- Letting people distract you.
- Inability to contain your anger.
- Tears from disappointing results.
- Letting people down.
- Distracting, irritating people.
- Bewildering unidentified stuff.
- Bad luck.
- That unexpected cold or illness.

We'll treat all of this stuff as crucial information that will help you learn how to navigate the good and bad moments of your game and, eventually, win. You simply identify stuff, fix it and move on.

We'll treat this component in Step 2 just like a GPS device in your vehicle. Even when you make a wrong turn, real GPS devices autocorrect for you to get you back in the right direction. With this program's GPS, you'll learn to autocorrect for yourself to get you back on track after mistakes and disasters and help you to stay there. We'll call this process of autocorrecting your iGPS (imaginary GPS), the second part of your operating system.

Step 4: Install and apply the tools of champions

In Step 4, you'll learn the tools that drive and support the system. These tools are applications that make sure your new system runs smoothly. You'll be learning powerful tools to fix stuff or blocks you identified and ensure you stay in high-performance mode. We'll call this bundle of tools iAPPs (imaginary applications). iAPPs represent the third and final piece of your operating system. You'll learn iAPPS to:

- Generate dynamite focus and visual acuity
- Gain huge levels of confidence and stop nervousness
- Forget embarrassing moments
- Help learn new skills fast
- Stop people from bothering you
- Make the target look bigger…and slower
- Feel taller, stronger and more adrenalized

Step 5: Run your high-performance system

In STEP 5, you experience how your operating system (vSELFIE, iGPS and iAPPs) starts to work automatically with practice, because the more you practice setting goals, identifying blocks and fixing them with your new applications, the sooner your game gets better, simpler, and "winninger."

All the tools you learn start to work automatically and effortlessly without you having to think. This is your operating system:

Step 2: You set and intensify your goals for winning

Step 3: You identify the blocks that happen to frustrate your attempts to win

Step 4: You apply your tools and fix these blocks to winning

And voila! With practice, your system (Step 5) comes together with greater and greater effectiveness and efficiency.

Step 6: Strive for excellence

Step 6 is up to you. It is not so much a step as it is all about empowering yourself to be a leader in your game and in life. As you move through the book, you'll start to fill in the little squares on the cell phone diagram with specific operations and applications to demonstrate how the system runs as efficiently and smoothly as your cell phone.

Throughout the book, I'll give you some tasks to do so that you can practice all the tools. I promise that they'll be easy tasks, because I know that you are busy with training and going to school and need a little time left over to socialize with friends. Trust me. What I'm teaching will make your game more fun, give you an advantage over your competitors and maybe give you extra time to practice or socialize more.

All I ask from you is for you to learn and apply this system as you set out to become a champion, as fast as possible, maybe in a year or two. Some people might call this unrealistic, but I would call it what my athletes do on a regular basis. And you are now one of my athletes. This is not about being realistic; it's about becoming a champion.

Skill Drill 1: Create your dream

Before the next chapter, I have one task for you to do, and I promise that you can do it in five minutes. Make a list of what you want in your clays game. I've given you an example in the box below.

WISH LIST FOR YOUR CLAYS GAME

- Win competitions
- Win a junior title
- Beat everyone at your club
- Lead your teammates and high-school friends to a championship
- Win a world or Olympic championship
- Get top grades in school

Here are some starter words:

- *Win...*
- *Achieve ...*
- *Create ...*
- *Get more skillful at ...*
- *Improve my grades or GPA to ...*

It's a good idea to get this list done asap. You can create a list of your goals or simply start thinking of them. Most of you have them already. Then turn the page and we'll get started helping you to prepare for the rest of your competitive life with the first step—turning the system ON with what we will call your GO-ZONE start button. I, personally, can't wait to see how soon you'll be crushing clays consistently and on the pathway to winning.

Training Tip

The goal lists you create will be an ongoing, yearly process. At some point in your sporting life, coaches will ask you to start a journal and keep track of goals (and problems and patterns of missed targets).

Right now, I'm just happy you are thinking about and reading this book to help you achieve your goals (and dreams).

TEEN vs TARGET PLAYBOOK

STEP 1

IGNITE YOUR HIGH-PERFORMANCE MIND

THE GO-ZONE

This is the fire in your heart that you trigger as the ON button.
It engages your high-performance mind and body
with supercharged energy—every time you step into the stand.

> *Experience is a hard teacher because she gives the test first, the lesson afterward.*
>
> **— VERNON LAW,**
> Star Baseball Pitcher

2
BE AN ARCHAEOLOGIST

Dig for high-performance gold.

> " *"If you have everything under control, you're not moving fast enough.*
>
> **— MARIO ANDRETTI,**
> <small>STAR RACE CAR DRIVER</small> "

Make sure you have listed your goals on paper or in your head. Be bold (even "unrealistic"), as at your age you have likely no idea how good you can be and how good you can eventually become.

So, winning a competition and/or helping yourself or your team win at a championship should be high on your list. Getting a college degree, apprenticeship or career of some sort should be on the list as well.

You have entered Step 1, where starting your high-performance (winning) machine will be as easy as turning on your cell phone. This "ON" button starts everything—intense focus, the slowing down of targets, the disappearance of distractions, the disappearance of people. Imagine only seeing the targets and blocking out the typical competition chaos. Excitingly, this leads to inkballed target after inkballed target. Also called consistency. And, eventually, winning.

Very likely and quickly, this "ON" button is going to change your game. You'll quickly notice. Others will notice too. Your coach will notice. Your parents will notice. Your competitors will notice. Because this "ON" button will fire you up from the get-go, giving you your own little secret as to why you are standing out.

Getting to the top of the leaderboard

I'm going to show you how to stand out now and be a leader.

Right now. Today.

And that doesn't mean you'll be a *show-off* to your opponents or your squadmates. But you will be a *show-how* as you will show them *how* to perform well, be consistent and win.

I learned this way back when I was a young athlete. Not in hockey, as my opponents would beat me before I even started the game by intimidating me. And that would completely throw me off, with my skills evaporating.

But it was in the sport of karate where I learned a new way, and this way will change everything about your game and maybe your whole life, just as it did mine. It will make standing out and standing up for yourself easy.

This "ON" button is called being in the GO-ZONE.

Dig for gold

During moments of pure brilliance in your game, you feel unstoppable. I call this unstoppable feeling or "ON" button, the GO-ZONE. It is dazzling and exciting and the main reason you love playing sports and winning.

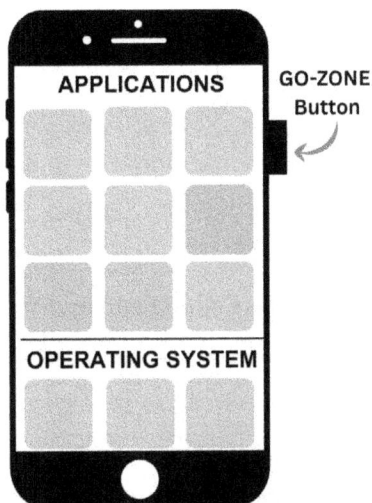

APPLICATIONS

GO-ZONE Button

OPERATING SYSTEM

By getting your GO-ZONE feeling to come to the surface, you just know that your game is "ON" and that you'll win. But when this good feeling stays hidden under the debris of self-doubt and failure, you feel "OFF," discouragement sets in, negative thoughts weigh you down and you just know that you'll lose.

So now, it will be your job to uncover the GO-ZONE feeling so that you ensure you stay in it all of the time. Because, believe it or not, that GO-ZONE feeling is your "ON" button for winning and success.

To discover your GO-ZONE, I'm going to ask you to be an archaeologist of sorts. Archaeologists dig with a trowel through layers of soil in search of important and ancient artifacts—like Aztec gold antiquities.

You'll need to dig through your past, gritty (unpleasant) memories of competitions, "scrape away" the dirt (of misses and embarrassments) and rediscover your solidly golden rounds with brilliantly smoked targets. Maybe you crushed a 25 straight! Maybe you dusted a few targets in a row! Maybe you only smoked one target, right in the sweet spot! But with that success you felt great. You felt amazing. You felt euphoric. You may have felt electric. Warm. Expansive. Taller.

Now, focus on just one priceless solid-gold memory of a success, and ignore all the dirt (the lousy times when you missed targets as we'll work on them later). Go ahead and feel it.

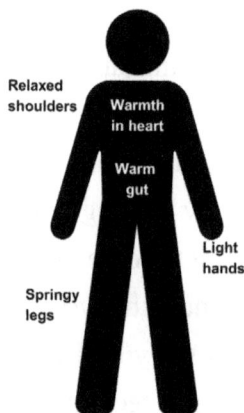

GO-ZONE

Relaxed shoulders

Warmth in heart

Warm gut

Light hands

Springy legs

- There's a smile on your face.
- Your heart is thumping faster.
- The core of your body is warm like you've just eaten a hot bowl of soup.
- Your legs are springier like being on a trampoline.
- Your hands and arms feel tingly and relaxed.

Similar to this list of sensations, drill down into the interior sensations of your chest area (core) as you think of the success. Notice the sensations that your priceless artifact (memory) generates. In your gut. Around your core. Throughout your neck, shoulders, spine.

The sensations have always been there, believe it not, but you've just missed them in the past. Now's your chance to not only notice them, but really notice them and turn them into your "ON" button for winning. And once you do that, everything changes. Like everything.

Skill Drill 2: Green-light signal for blastoff

1. **Make a list of three experiences** where you were at your brilliant best and, one at a time, imagine how each felt.

2. **Drill down and notice what and where you feel certain sensations**—in your heart, core, gut, back, neck, arms and legs.

3. **Then go stand in front of the bathroom mirror and notice what you look like when you feel these sensations.** Trust me, you'll be impressed. And trust me, that is what your competitors will now see when you take that feeling to the stand.

With this very specific feeling, you have done a masterful job of being an archaeologist and discovered your GO-ZONE. You now have the means to turn your high-performance system to "ON." As they say when a rocket launches, "Houston, we have liftoff."

Next up

In the next chapter, we'll look at why this first step of the GO-ZONE is so important and how you'll actually use it in your shooting game.

Training Tip

Use the chart below, with three columns, as a guide for discovering your GO-ZONE. Remember each memory, and list the sensations you felt. Then pick the strongest and most obvious sensation as your GO-ZONE.

1st GO-ZONE Sensation	2nd GO-ZONE Sensation	3rd GO-ZONE Sensation
✓ Breathing is faster		
✓ Posture is more erect		
✓ Arms and hands light		
✓ Chest expansive		
✓ Electricity in chest		
✓ Abdomen feels solid		

3
ENGINEER YOUR ZONE

Refine your pure-gold experiences.

66

Winning isn't everything, but wanting it is.

— ARNOLD PALMER,
STAR GOLFER

99

You have now dabbled in archaeology, dug down deep into your brilliant memories of success and discovered the means for a lifelong ability to perform at the highest levels, a sensation called the GO-ZONE. Now, let's put it to use.

Sure, you might say, I have discovered that wonderful and very distinct feeling in my gut (heart, core, neck or hands) when I think of past golden experiences, but how does that relate to tomorrow's practice or next week's competition? The answer is simple and we'll stop being an archaeologist and start thinking like an engineer.

What we did is called *reverse engineering*, which is the act of dismantling an object to see how it works. It is done primarily to analyze and gain knowledge about the way something works, but in our case we'll use it to duplicate an object.

For example, if you wished to construct a cell phone, you'd buy one, totally disassemble it, identify the component parts and study how it's put together. And then you'd separately manufacture all the components, put them back together on an assembly line and, voila, you have a new cell phone. Now, because of reverse-engineering, you can create a million phones.

In your role as archaeologist, you uncovered a brilliant memory of success (the object). You took the memory apart by noticing how it felt in your body (disassembled it), and you discovered some very interesting components (sensations such as warmth in your core, for example). This is the inner workings of that memory, just as the wires and silicone chips are the inner workings of the cell phone.

Now, just as you could imagine reconstructing one or a million cell phones from the one you took apart, you can reconstruct a million GO-ZONEs by reconstructing that warmth in your core and essentially, putting that memory back together. By consciously thinking of (and reconstructing) that warmth in your core, you can build one new GO-ZONE. And then, nothing is stopping you from making a million of them. Try it.

The impact of being in your GO-ZONE

Just by thinking of that warmth in your core, stuff happens. You'll actually notice yourself standing up straighter. You'll notice a burst of adrenaline. You'll notice your mind going quiet with no self-talk. You'll feel stronger, more alert, more aware. This reassembled GO-ZONE ensures that you are prepared for the next shot, round or competition. And it is just as available as any other part of your equipment.

With loads of practice, it will become your normal way of performing in your sport and life.

From here on in, this kind of good feeling is going to be your "green light." It starts your system, your GO-ZONE! Feel this sensation, step into the stand, execute your pre-shot routine and pull the trigger.

Warm feeling in your gut. **PULL!**

Adrenalized feeling in your core. **PULL!**

Tingles in your neck and shoulders. **PULL!**

Find your one (only one!) internal GO-ZONE sensation and you'll surely reassemble your past moment of brilliance. **PULL!**

The way to win gold—your GO-ZONE signal

With practice (and with the remainder of this book), you will learn to be consistent with your fully developed GO-ZONE in everything you do. The secret is out, for you at least. This pleasant GO-ZONE sensation tells you that everything is a "go." Spend some good old archaeological and reverse-engineering time on this. Take the lead and show everyone *how* to be a champion—and, with your GO-ZONE, stand out from your opponents.

As a recap:

1. **Play archaeologist and sift through the dirt of your bad rounds** to discover your golden moments when you had a 25 straight, a few smoked targets in a row or one absolute ink ball. (In upcoming chapters you'll learn to discard the dirt of all the dropped birds, and learn a lot from that process).

2. **Notice what those golden moments of success feel like**—ie. more energy, faster heartbeat, warmth in your chest, overall lightness (bounce in your legs).

3. **Be the engineer and reverse engineer your GO-ZONE. Take one of your sensations (just one) and use it like a "green light" signal** telling you that it is okay to step into the stand and go for gold! It starts your system; it starts everything.

Skill Drill 3: Build super powers

Your skill drill now is to ensure you feel your GO-ZONE every time you step into the stand, in practice and in competition. Whether you are in-season or in the off-season break, use your GO-ZONE for all of your training from dryland training to visualizing winning shoot-offs.

You also need to be in your GO-ZONE in school, for listening, taking notes and writing tests. And at home, apply it to your homework and chores. Apply it everywhere, even to tasks you find boring or dislike, as even they will seem a lot easier and perhaps more pleasant. It is your "ON" button.

Next up

This is the end of archaeology and reverse-engineering, and it is the start of you becoming a champion. In the next chapter, I'll give you a way to practice your GO-ZONE to ensure you can really feel it and really make it work for you.

Training Tip

If you struggle to find the gold-nugget memories in the dust of your clays' experiences, examine other areas of your life. Like cycling or ATVing or dirt-bike riding. Or other school sports or crafts. Or music or art. Or equestrian riding.

Life is full of great GO-ZONE experiences. As an archaeologist, you may have to have a keen eye to identify them, but you'll know they are real gold artifacts by how good they feel.

"

Good, better, best. Never let it rest. Until your good is better and your better is best.

— TIM DUNCAN,
STAR BASKETBALL PLAYER

"

4
UNLEASH HIGH PERFORMANCE

Test out your Zone.

> " *You've got to take the initiative and play your game. In a decisive game, the Zone is the difference.* "
>
> **— CHRIS EVERT,**
> STAR TENNIS PLAYER

I have introduced you to your green-light feeling for the GO-ZONE—a sensation in your core or in your shoulders or in your legs—a feeling for absolute readiness that you've identified and now need to practice. It is personal.

This chapter will give you an opportunity to apply it outside of your sport. And then, through practicing it in your sport, it will become very obvious and improve the consistency of your performance.

Now, maybe some of you are reading this chapter without having gotten your sensation for the GO-ZONE. Please, pause your reading here and go back to Chapter 2. Take some time to first identify your GO-ZONE and then come back here so you can apply this absolutely important, critical, necessary and success-reliant part of your game.

Based on my many years of competing in karate and working with athletes in many sports and at all levels of sport, having the GO-ZONE is like having a light switch. When I could turn it "ON," I'd generally find a route to the podium.

I congratulate those of you who have already noticed a difference in your confidence based on your new GO-ZONE signal. In this chapter, you get to apply your GO-ZONE without the need to be at the range. I call it the Own the Zone exercise and you'll require three things:

1. A ball (a tight bundle of socks will also do)
2. A waste basket, and,
3. A room big enough to toss the ball where there is nothing that can be broken.

You'll also need your green-light feeling of the GO-ZONE and an oversized imagination for winning a cool brand-new cell phone (with all the latest features).

Part A: Own the Zone exercise

1. **Stand right over the basket and, in order to win an imaginary cell phone, drop the ball into the basket.** Sounds easy and it is! You win! Notice how your GO-ZONE is clear, strong and very pleasant—with no thinking! **But we are going to make it more difficult.**

2. **Back away three big steps and notice how your GO-ZONE fades slightly as you step backward.** Maybe a bit of self-talk happens and a little doubt occurs, but you stretch forward and toss the ball into the basket for a second cell phone, and win one for your friend! (Ka-ching!) **But let's make it even more difficult.**

3. **From that point, step backward another three big steps and notice how your GO-ZONE fades further** and maybe there is more doubt and more self-talk and you hit the basket or maybe you don't. (A buzzer sounds when you miss and someone "unfollows" you.)

4. **One more time, from that point, move back an impossible three more big steps and notice how your GO-ZONE fades away,** perhaps entirely, and there's a very good likelihood that you miss the basket. No more cell phones for you or your friends.

But that is only the start of the exercise. The point here is to show you that typically your cell phone-winning GO-ZONE melts into nothingness the further you get away from the basket. You sink into what I call the NO-ZONE (which appropriately rhymes with no phone.) It could be argued that the occasional successful basket at greater distances might evoke a shot of adrenaline and a resurgence of your Zone. True, but I wouldn't bet on it.

Part B: Own the Zone exercise

No matter how many steps you move away from the basket, you will need to sustain your GO-ZONE to ensure success. So, let's try it again. In Part B, you'll learn to hang on tightly to your cell phone-winning GO-ZONE in the same way you'll ultimately apply it to every time you step into the stand and pull the trigger:

1. **Once again, hovering right over the basket and for an imaginary cell phone prize, drop the ball into the basket.** Just as easy as last time! Your GO-ZONE is clear, strong and feeling good.

2. **This time *before* moving backward, stand right over the basket, recapture your cell phone-winning GO-ZONE** and maintain it as you step backward three big steps. Now throw the ball with your GO-ZONE. Congratulations, that should give you a feeling for what we are after here.

3. **Next, again *before* moving backward, stand right over the basket, recapture your cell phone-winning GO-ZONE** and step backward six big steps and maintain the cell-phone winning feeling. Keep it strong and intense. Now throw the ball while feeling it. Congratulations again if you maintained it, even if you missed the basket.

4. **And one last time, again *before* moving backward, stand right over the basket, recapture your cell phone-winning GO-ZONE,** and, with that feeling maintained, step backward nine big steps and again throw the ball while in your GO-ZONE.

Congratulations! Your GO-ZONE should be getting way more obvious and way easier to sustain.

No fear, no thinking and no self-talk

When I take young athletes through Part A of the Own the Zone exercise they are careful and frequently miss, likely because they are thinking of winning (or losing) the cell phone. I can see the added stress on their faces, where, even though the prize is imaginary, they are totally obsessed with hitting the basket (and winning).

Some would say that they need to "focus on technique rather than winning." But no, technique is not an issue with throwing the ball. Rather, they need to focus on their GO-ZONE (which represents them at their best with no thinking and no fear).

In Part B of the Own the Zone exercise, when you are only focused on the good feeling of your GO-ZONE and not thinking of anything else, your success should go way up as there is no fear, no thinking and no self-talk. As a matter of fact, my clients rarely miss.

Skill Drill 3: Test out your GO-ZONE

Now I want you to test out both parts of the Own the Zone exercise. And then I want you to apply this same approach to your clays game.

1. **Get your GO-ZONE** (in your gut, chest, shoulders, etc.) before you get out of the car at the range and then stay with the feeling while you assemble your equipment and put on your vest. (As you move further in the program, you'll learn the tools to build your extreme ability to sustain it.)

2. **Then, stay with that great feeling** as you walk to the range.

3. **And then, stay with it as you step into the stand,** do your pre-shot routine and call *pull*.

4. **Same for the next stand.**

5. **Continue in this manner from stand to stand, round to round**—and for the rest of your competitive life.

You will lose the GO-ZONE from time to time, for a number of reasons:

- Someone gives you advice just before you start your round and it creates a distraction or over-thinking.
- A friend interrupts your game and chats with you before you begin.
- The wind is blowing hard and people ahead of you are missing targets and you start thinking about the wind.
- You forget to turn your phone off and a text distracts you.
- You miss a target or two, think others are laughing at you and spiral downward.

But you must get it back, as every time you get your GO-ZONE back, your game starts to improve. It is a feel thing, and it is a necessary part of learning to win as your GO-ZONE starts to become automatic.

Play with your GO-ZONE and practice it in clays, in school and in everything you do. And one of the best ways to practice your GO-ZONE is with the Own the Zone exercise. Set up the basket and have some fun throwing your balled-up socks into it— in your GO-ZONE and loving everything about the way it feels!

Next up

Yes, we all struggle to get into our GO-ZONE at times and we may lose it from time to time (especially early in the program). In the next chapter you will learn Step 2 in this system so that you can resolve one of the biggest reasons for losing your GO-ZONE— pre-game nervousness—by adding a unique way of thinking about goal setting and visualization as a part of your operating system. You'll learn to banish nervousness forever, but first, spend a little more time practicing your GO-ZONE and make it feel like, well, normal.

Training Tip

After you try the Own the Zone exercise a couple of times, put pressure on yourself by challenging a friend to see who can get the most baskets. This kind of friendly competition actually works to help you deal with competition pressure so you love it, as it too begins to feel normal.

"

Visualization fuels the fire within, igniting the pursuit of excellence.

— JERRY MICULEK,
STAR COMPETITIVE SHOOTER

"

TEEN vs TARGET PLAYBOOK

STEP 2

SUPERCHARGE YOUR SPORT VISION

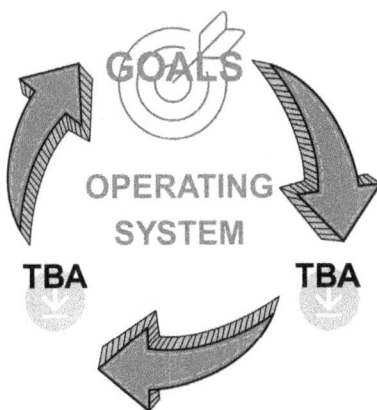

Just as your cell phone has an operating system, you do too. This is where you will be entering the first key part of it—your goals. They represent what you want—the win, high GPA marks, new friends.

Most importantly, as impossible as it may seem to some of you who feel sick from being nervous at times or most of the time, you're going to learn to banish nervousness forever. Just wait and read on, as you'll soon get to test it out for yourself.

"

Visualization is the bridge that connects dreams to reality.

— NICCOLO CAMPRIANI,
STAR SHOOTING COACH

"

5
DIAL IN FOR SUCCESS

Make winning a 'done deal'.

" "

You can't put a limit on anything.
The more you dream, the farther you get.

— **MICHAEL PHELPS,**
Star Swimmer

" "

You have learned the first part of the formula—your GO-ZONE. You now have that feeling in your chest or gut or shoulders that tells you that you are ready to compete. When you feel it, you need to trust that you are ready. You can check in on it at any time. Before you step into the stand. Before you call pull. The ball and basket exercise will highlight your GO-ZONE to such a degree that you'll be itching to test your GO-ZONE out on the range.

In this chapter, you have entered Step 2, and are going to put your nerves in a basket as well, and be done with them. When I played hockey, my stomach turned upside down before games. I felt like I was going to be sick and I thought, hey, everyone must feel this awful before competing.

I think that most of my teammates felt the same way and you can imagine what a mess of emotions the locker room was. Awful! Only now, I know that it was *not* normal and should never be considered normal. Had I known about the GO-ZONE and how to get ready to compete instead of accepting nervousness as normal, my game would have been way different and way more fun.

I should have felt excited as I was putting on my hockey equipment and entered the game prepared. Sadly, that was not the case. And unfortunately, it typically took me two full periods (40 minutes) to get into my best game. If I was lucky, I experienced a random moment in the GO-ZONE. For you, that would be like going through two full rounds at the range before you even felt warmed up. Imagine how many mistakes you would make. You'd be chipping away at targets with no assurance that you'd get any of them. You deserve better. You deserve to be ready.

When I typically ask athletes to think about an upcoming competition, they give me a deer-in-the-headlights look of nervous uncertainty as to how they expect they'll perform. At that point I jump in and say,

"You gotta know you'll win."

Some athletes push back and tell me that winning is less important than skill development. They've been told to focus on skills rather than outcome, as focusing on winning just makes them nervous and they perform even worse. Blah, blah, blah. I hear it all the time.

But then I ask them why they play the game. I get answers like:

To get better; to be more skillful; to be more consistent…

And then I put it all together and ask, what will happen in your game when you get better, more skillful and more consistent? Sometimes it takes a little teeth pulling but I always get a sheepish:

"I want to win."

The reality is that we are all in the game to win. Don't let anyone tell you otherwise. It is important to learn how to win (as well as to learn how to lose). And now I'm going to teach you how to win by properly visualizing your upcoming competition by upleveling your adrenaline into a super-tsunami of power.

You'll be turning an imaginary cell phone camera on yourself and creating a visualized selfie of the future. It's a highly GO-ZONE'd version where you see yourself winning absolutely everything. And it's called a vSELFIE (visualized SELFIE).

Set up your vSELFIE

Selfies, as you know, capture you in a moment in time. When you play it back, it is a past moment in time. But that's boring. So let's change it up. What if you could take a selfie of your future and that future selfie was you being fabulously successful in that future competition?

Before that competition, for example, you could watch yourself hitting absolutely every target, composed, adrenalized, powerful, focused and in the GO-ZONE. That's quite a change from past competitions where you likely doubted that you'd do well. When you create your vSELFIE of your next competition in this manner,

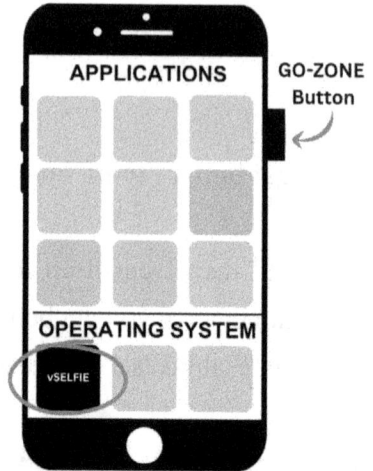

you kind of feel that you already won it, even though it hasn't even happened yet.

The impact on you watching your future success feels amazingly good and gives you incredible confidence. Because, unlike your peers, you can see and feel your future success in full color and dynamic action. You look good, skillful and confident, plus you see yourself on the podium!

And not only have you won, but by repeating the vSELFIE a hundred or more times, you feel like you have won a hundred or more competitions. Imagine your euphoria and confidence when you arrive at your competition. Sure, be a bit skeptical, because it surely isn't real. Go ahead and pinch yourself. But amazingly, it feels real, partly by adding crazy amounts of adrenaline and partly by repetition.

Now, in the following vSELFIE exercise, let's do it. Let's create your bright selfie future so you can watch it a few hundred times to see and feel what is going to happen at your next competition. Winning might just feel like a done deal!

Visualize with your vSELFIE

1. **Find a quiet place to sit and close your eyes with NO parents, siblings or friends hanging around to bother you.** Power up your GO-ZONE. (It might be a good idea to power off or mute your cell phone for just a few minutes to avoid being distracted.)

2. **You'll now need to add some adrenaline. Lots of it.** I used to dance around my recreation room and pretend that I was sparring with an imaginary opponent. This is called *shadow boxing* and it may help you build up your adrenaline level. Get up from your chair and jump up and down, hoot and holler and do what it takes to feel really excited. With high adrenaline, you get high impact!

3. **Once your adrenaline is pressure-cooker high, imagine yourself on an imaginary, arms-length phone screen.** You are now imagining a future selfie of you performing well and winning. This is a *v*SELFIE of you in the GO-ZONE crushing clay target after clay target. Keeping your adrenaline amplified, watch yourself pulverize the targets. Admire your amazing skill. And remember, with high adrenaline, you get high impact!

4. **After about 60 seconds of watching your *v*SELFIE-self crush clays, imagine stepping onto the screen and being that person.** Physically raise your hands like you are aiming at the target. Feel high levels of adrenaline running through your body. Call *pull* and feel yourself pull the trigger. In this manner, for the next 60 seconds

experience the future success with full audio. And again, with high adrenaline, you get high impact.

5. **Now step back off of your *v*SELFIE screen and take another look at your successful image.** Notice how much fun you're having. Especially notice the power of your GO-ZONE feeling inside you, as it may now be epic!

6. **Repeat this *v*SELFIE visualization a couple of more times now, right away, and then later in your day.** One of my clients visualizes her vSELFIE every morning after a shower. Another visualizes on the way to practices when his parents drive him. Take the time to visualize your vSELFIE and do it frequently, perhaps four or five times a day.

This kind of practice is front-end loaded. In other words, the more vSELFIEs you do this way now, the fewer you may have to do before upcoming competitions, as being in your GO-ZONE with elevated adrenaline will start to feel like a normal part of winning. Your vSELFIE will help you to change your game and I'm guessing that you now understand why you will never feel nervous again.

I like to equate your shooting performance to brain surgery. With multiple surgeries already completed, surgeons perform operations with full confidence. I find it hard to believe that they would be nervous.

Nervousness in any job or sport is abnormal and nothing we have to accept or accommodate. The feeling of winning needs to be normal. And, as you now know, by adding high-adrenaline levels to your vSELFIE, you get high performance with high impact! And that should be your new normal.

Skill Drill 5: Love training with your vSELFIE

When I first used my vSELFIE in karate, in my mind I won all of my competitions before I even got to the venue, with full adrenaline. Did I actually win them all? Well, no. But I felt like I was going to and I did win most of them. I still kind of smile and think I won them all.

The pregame nervousness of hockey was a thing of the past and the euphoria of competing was everywhere—*in my karate training, in my running and wind sprints and during my travel to the competitions.*

I absolutely loved all parts of competing, especially meeting people and making new friends and then blocking all that out and playing to win. My *v*SELFIE was a huge part of it. And it has also got to be a huge part of your preparation for winning. Truly, the result will be zero nervousness. By the way, why are you in this game?

Next up

In the next chapter, I'll give you some tips for using your powerful *v*SELFIE in fun ways that will help you to overcome problems and fix mistakes before they become problems or mistakes. In the meantime, pull out and use your *v*SELFIE whenever you can. In the *v*SELFIE game, repetition matters.

Training Tip

When you visualize, you'll often see images quite differently from others. Some athletes see images in brilliant color. Some only see black and white images. Some see nothing but know that the imagined event is happening.

How you visualize does not matter, as long as you do it, and do it in an adrenalized manner. Some athletes ask me how many times a day they should do it. Lots, I say. Because it is front-end loaded, which means that the more you do it now, the less you'll have to do it later when you really get on a roll and are winning.

6
CREATE YOUR FUTURE

Follow Bob's five visualization rules.

66

Make each day your masterpiece.

— **JOHN WOODEN,**
STAR COACH

99

You have learned the foundation of your formula—the GO-ZONE—that feeling in your chest or gut or shoulders that tells you that you are ready to step into the stand and pull the trigger. And now you have learned the first part of your operating system with the ability to see the future and rehearse it with your imagination by using your vSELFIE. So, do you still want to be a champion? Let's keep going.

Several years ago, I worked with Olympic gold medalist Hannah Teter who would snowboard 30 or more feet in the air, do a gazillion McTwists and turns, and then land on her feet—most of the time. Except, once in a while she injured herself.

As jumping 30 feet in the air can be risky and scary, how did she train safely? Well, she visualized it first on her vSELFIE, that's how. Many, many, many times (add a thousand *manys*), before she ever did it at great height on packed snow and ice. She saved a lot of bruises, grief and concussions and rather enjoyed flying high like an eagle when she practiced painlessly.

Now, for you in the clays-crushing business, the only thing that gets bruised when you miss (or miss a whole bunch) is your self-esteem. And the only thing that gets concussed is your shoulder or cheek. But even then, avoiding bruises is good. And like Hannah, the key is to visualize success first with your vSELFIE—for everything you do. It is your ticket to winning.

And just like Hannah, you'll have to follow Bob's Five Visualization Rules:

1. **You need to be in the GO-ZONE when you visualize.** As you remember, in Chapter 2, your GO-ZONE is that wonderful feeling in your core, shoulders, arms or hands. How you feel when you visualize with your vSELFIE is how you'll feel when you step into the stand to turn targets into dust.

2. **You need to *feel* like you just drank two cans of a power drink.** Now that's wired! But you need to do it with real adrenaline—not the liquid energy-drink stuff, as that can be difficult to control and may result in inconsistency in your game.

   To get real adrenaline, try pretending to fight an imaginary shadow (called shadow boxing) or dance excitedly around your bedroom. Do everything you can physically to get wired with adrenaline before you watch your vSELFIE. IMPORTANT: How wired you feel with this kind of practice is how wired you'll be in the stand on competition day. Otherwise, you'll be way too-o-o-o-o-o calm-m-m-m-m (Z-z-z-z).

3. **Visualize in private.** When you do your *v*SELFIE, you'll make faces and move your arms in small ways, not to mention that your eyes will be moving underneath your eyelids as though you are dreaming. Ever seen a dog dream with its legs twitching as though it is trying to run? When you visualize properly, you may do the same thing.

On the funny side, you might be visualizing on your bus ride to school, with all the facial expressions and twitching of your hands as you visualize moving to and crushing a target, and when you open your eyes, the other kids on the bus are wide-eyed and cautious, and moving away from you to the other side of the bus.

In other words, when you properly visualize, you will look a little different and make movements that are normal but look random. So, just saying, do your *v*SELFIE in the privacy of your home or car.

4. **Keep your *v*SELFIE short but with high energy.** How long is your shot process (as timed from the squadmate going before you, to your shot)? Seconds? So you can keep your visualization short.

Ramp up your adrenaline, get in your GO-ZONE, and spend only a minute or so on each sequence. Then repeat the sequence. (For athletes in other sports such as gymnastics where specific floor routines may be minutes long, the visualization process can be extended.)

5. **Do lots of *v*SELFIE practice.** When you can't get to the range because it's cold, do your *v*SELFIE. Never been to a competition on a range that everyone tells you has hard-to-see targets? Go on the internet, locate an image of the range and imagine it as part of your *v*SELFIE. Never been in a shoot-off? Do your *v*SELFIE of one. Never won a championship and been on the podium? Do your *v*SELFIE and stand on it proudly.

Proper visualization gives you solid confidence, as though you've already won the championship a hundred or more times. As long as you follow rules 1 and 2 above, and do the visualization a hundred or so times, your brain will start to believe it is that easy.

Finally, I have gotten some questions on how detailed an athlete should make their vSELFIE. Personally, I'm no fan of detail. I like to watch and feel the big, bright, exciting video of success and let my subconscious mind fill in the blanks, often with a better result than if I had tried to program my karate fight second by second. This may change in some situations, so I'll leave it in your court and encourage you to figure out how much detail works for you.

Skill Drill 6: Visualize, visualize, visualize

So, there you go: Bob's Five Visualization Rules. While it is great practice to apply these vSELFIE rules to winning boldly, it is also important to apply them to tough situations, including competing on hot, rainy or windy days, recovering from misses, enjoying the pressure of shoot-offs (what pressure?), ignoring nasty competitors who try to distract you and dealing with equipment breakdowns.

Winston Churchill, the Prime Minister of Great Britain during World War II, once gave the shortest speech ever. "When do you quit?" he asked. "Never, never, never," was his answer. And then he sat down. I'll change up what he said:

How do you learn how to win and have fun?
Visualize, visualize, visualize!
But properly—with Bob's Five Visualization Rules
and your *v*SELFIE exercise.

And now I will sit down, be quiet and let you go and practice your *v*SELFIE a couple of hundred times. Visualize everything from winning competitions to performing well in high school and college courses in order to graduate with honors. You'll need to visualize many, many, many times in order to succeed, so that, like Hannah Teter, you'll land on your feet and not your head.

Next up

Have you ever heard that the immune system in young children gets stronger when they get sick from eating dirt? Well, to a degree at least. In the next chapter, you'll start the second part of your operating system, Step 3, where you'll learn that your ability to win gets stronger every time you miss a target or lose, especially when you use the right medicine or, in the case of this book, the right tools. You'll literally become immune to losing, and I promise that you won't have to deal with grit between your teeth.

Training Tip

All of your vSELFIEs don't need to be perfect rounds and perfect hits. As a matter of fact, be sure to throw in a few misses and watch how you perfectly crush the next targets.

Or, see your equipment malfunction and watch yourself deal with it like a pro. Or, watch how someone tries to distract you, and watch yourself pointing to your ear buds, smiling and walking away.

And then see yourself beat them in the competition. vSELFIEs are very good for empowering yourself in every area of your game, and life.

TEEN vs TARGET PLAYBOOK

STEP 3

NAVIGATE THE PRESSURES OF COMPETITION

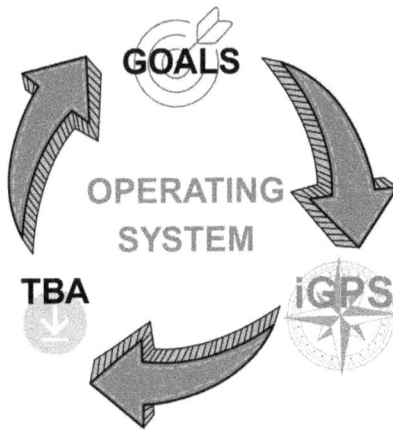

GPS is the next part of your operating system that allows you to navigate through problems and frustrations without beating yourself up too much.

Both the solid hits and embarrassing misses are a part of learning to win.

"

*Difficulties in life are intended
to make us better, not bitter.*

— DAN REEVES,
Star Football Coach

"

7
BE A NAVIGATOR

Operate your internal GPS
to guide you to success.

Now that you have your GO-ZONE and the first part of your operating system, your vSELFIE, we'll look at the second part of your operating system, the guidance system that will keep you on track. No, you are not a drone, but you do have a kind of internal GPS guidance system that will help you shoot like a machine.

You have now started on Step 3, where you are going to set up your own internal guidance device. It will be just like the GPS device that is on your cell phone that talks to you and guides you to your destination with a turn-by-turn commentary along your route. "Turn right. Turn left. Go straight. You missed the turn! Make the next available U-turn."

Over the last few years since the introduction of GPS, thousands of broken cell phones with GPS programs have been found lying on the roadside battered and bashed to pieces. Impatient drivers have become increasingly unglued when their cell phone GPS programs make mistakes, especially when the voice on the GPS gets downright sarcastic. So drivers have reportedly been grabbing their cell phones without thinking and chucking them out the window.

Of course, I'm telling a fib here, but only to make a point. GPS programs do make mistakes from time to time, but they self-correct, without people angrily tossing their cell phones from moving vehicles.

But each of us has a kind of *internal (mental)* GPS that helps us to act on the feedback of a missed target or a meltdown. As we human perfectionists get rather fussy about missing and will often beat ourselves up when we miss, iGPS changes everything and allows you to treat mistakes as exciting learning opportunities to keep you on track, just as your cell-phone program keeps you heading in the right direction.

Emotions are simply GPS

Beating yourself up after mistakes is okay. We all do it. But keep the beatings short and private, as public displays are rarely pleasant, and prolonging the emotions can result in additional mistakes and keep you from being resilient or self-correcting.

Your anger, frustration and embarrassment does you in and can cause you to fall into the death spiral of misses upon misses.

But, by treating these emotions as simply iGPS (internal feedback to be acted upon), you can adapt quickly and are better equipped to learn, develop and win. The destructive force creating multiple misses is gone. iGPS gets you back in the game. Ultimately, with practice, it autocorrects your game for you.

Keep in mind that this is a systems approach, not a psychological or emotional approach. In this model, treating emotions as curious obstacles to performance (iGPS) and not some kind of character trait you need to speak with a therapist about, makes resolving them so much easier (as you can do it without being emotional, and, most importantly, you can do it by yourself).

Thinking back to the idea of being an archaeologist might help. When you were looking for gold memories, you scraped away a lot of dirt. Most of your "emotional" outbursts are only iGPS dirt!

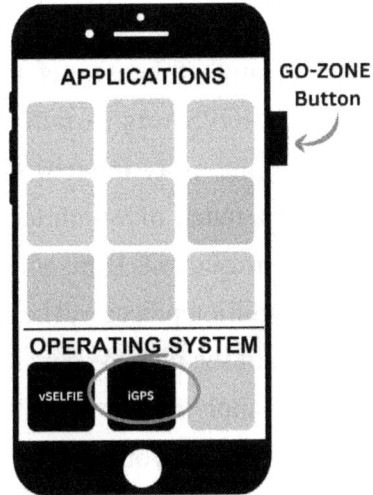

Case study: An athlete's game struggle

One of my athletes was very consistent in practice, but his personal iGPS was in tatters much of the time in competition. And oh, the nasty internal self-talk that echoed in his head after mistakes, much of which labeled him as stupid, incompetent and an embarrassment. If his iGPS resetting program existed at all, it lay in a million pieces by the roadside, or at the very least, glitching because of the names he was calling himself.

By applying his GO-ZONE and vSELFIE, as well as the other strategies you'll learn in this program, he debriefed every competition, identified the blocks that resulted in negative self-talk and then fixed them. As with most athletes in this process, he became very consistent.

Still, a perfect score in a round continued to elude him. He'd drop the first target and roll his eyes, or drop some random target in the middle and cuss under his breath, or drop the last target and really lose it and throw things. At one competition when he really, really, really lost it, I got wind of his behavior through one of my students and we had "the talk."

He did not know where that anger was coming from, so we turned his game upside down looking for the culprit iGPS. And when we actually identified it, we were both a little shocked and surprised. The block had nothing to do with his clays or any sport for that matter!

Many years ago, he and his high school choir had performed a concert in a "once in a lifetime" venue. But horror upon horror, the orchestra screwed up on them and they received a devastating review in the media by a critic who called the performance stupid, incompetent and an embarrassment.

As a result, he'd felt very angry at the time. And, now, many years later, that anger seeped to the surface and created doubt. And with doubt came the inevitable miss and a loss. His GO-ZONE disappeared—all because of archaeological iGPS anger from years earlier.

Once he identified it, he plugged into a number of strategies and got his GO-ZONE back. Soon after, he achieved his perfect score. More importantly, because of the many iGPS corrections he had made and continues to make, his subconscious mind has truly mastered the art of iGPS auto-correcting.

Skill Drill 7: Wrong turns corrected

When you learn to see problems as simply wrong turns or iGPS, resolving them is way easier as they bear no emotional baggage. No longer are you angry, frustrated, embarrassed or disappointed. Well, maybe a little, but in the end you now know it's the kind of iGPS that will help guide you to vast improvements and maybe even a championship.

Each finished competition presents exciting opportunities to fix newly revealed iGPS. Not that you want it to happen, but getting good at fixing it is what we refer to as resiliency. And slowly but surely, your game starts to become way more fun.

Next up

By maintaining your GO-ZONE, you have learned to power up your system. And by practicing your vSELFIE over and over as the vision of your game and by using iGPS consistently to keep you on track, you are continually improving your game and developing your operating system for winning.

Soon, you'll start learning the very powerful tools to get yourself back on track when you lose your GO-ZONE. But first, just to be sure that you (and your parents) fully understand how and why iGPS works, we need to look at why competing (with both the wins and losses) is so very, very important on your journey to becoming a champion.

Training Tip

Start treating all of your mistakes as simply iGPS. Every time you miss a target, take a second and immediately re-visualize that target and crush it.

This one second of your time is invaluable as it will do three things:

1. It will ensure you only remember the target being crushed (not the miss).

2. It will likely resolve any technical issue if there is one.

3. It will ultimately develop into a reflex where problems get fixed automatically.

8
BE A SCIENTIST

Treat every competition as a high-performance experiment.

> ❝
> *If you don't fall, how are you going to know what getting up is like?*
>
> **— STEPH CURRY,**
> Star Basketball Player
> ❞

You have come so far with your game (in only seven chapters). You know to look for that sensation of your GO-ZONE as your starting point. You know how to build powerful goals by vSELFIE practice—especially by adding adrenaline—as part of your operating system.

And you have the ability to uplevel your operating system by treating mistakes and losses as guidance with your iGPS, just like a cell phone GPS device guides you to your destination. Now, we'll look at how your competitions (both winning and losing) are like a grand science experiment that allows you to find the perfect winning formula.

I've seen so many parents get upset at their teen's competition results.

Drop a final shot? Sad parent.
Have a bad round? Sad parent.
Have a bad day? Sad parent.

Now, if this reminds you of how your parents behave, sad parents are not bad parents. Mostly they care *too* much. They are attached to you, of course. They love you. They want you to succeed.

And the reason it causes trouble is that you are unable to tell if they are sad *for* you (disappointed and feeling your pain of losing) or sad *because* of you (disappointed that you failed to follow what they or your coach said). The look on their faces and the sagging of their shoulders looks the same, either way.

But the biggest difficulty with your parents' emotions is that you have a direct emotional connection with them—faster than high-speed broadband, fiber optics internet with booster capacity. When you have had a bad moment such as dropping a string of targets, they *feel* your pain instantly. And you turn around and see them frowning (in pain), and instantly your pain doubles, because you *feel* theirs.

And then theirs quadruples as they feel your pain. In seconds, you have a runaway train of connected emotions of pain, with ever increasing levels of pain. (In an upcoming chapter you'll learn what causes this, but for now, trust me that it is a thing.)

The importance of game skills

It is important for you and your parents to know that there are three key skills that you need to learn in order to become a champion: Technical skills, mental skills and game skills. All are key, but the last one is often messy—game skills. Because you must compete in order to learn how to win. It is a skill that takes practice and patience, and like science experiments, you'll fail a lot in order to get better at winning.

So, please forget the disappointment piece! Instead, it is a time for everyone to get excited that you were brave enough to put yourself on the line and practice your game skills in a competition. You are pitting yourself against your peers, the weather, new ranges and inconsistent targets where anything can go wrong. And it often does, with the experiment blowing up in your face!

Game skills are the skills that you can *only* learn in a game by putting yourself on the line, head to head with other competitors, and allow *stuff* to affect you, over and over (iGPS) until you figure it out. For example, the crush of officials, coaches and athletes causes your heart to race, and you tighten up and feel sick.

Seeing top athletes dressed in National-Team vests causes you to breathe shallowly as grave doubts about your skills creep in. You fret about the score and it draws you to the leaderboard to see where you stand—good or bad—and your shoulders droop as you look in disbelief. You accidentally see a squadmate miss an easy target and a flash of fear flashes through your body that predicts that you'll miss too.

These are real game examples and you can experiment by recreating these pressures during practices and pretend that you are good at overcoming them. More than likely they, and unexpected other ones, will pop up at competitions in ways you could never expect.

So you have to expect the unexpected, and get good at dealing with unexpected pressures during the competition and practices. Here are three things to consider as you play scientist and experiment in your competitions:

1. **Competing is good for you and your game as it reveals chinks in your armor (iGPS).** The following are some real ongoing learnings from competitions:

   - Forgetting his shotgun at home on one occasion, an athlete created a checklist of items he needed to bring to competitions in order to be confident that he had all of his kit together.
   - Struggling with sleepiness and inability to maintain focus, an athlete learned that playing computer games late into the night was counterproductive to winning the next day.
   - Dealing with sore and dry eyes in his event, an athlete made a habit of resting her eyes during the last hour of her ride to competitions.
   - Feeling angry after missing several targets on an awful, frigid day, an athlete found, to his surprise, that he was sitting in second place. It taught him to love bad weather, because he knew that when he missed a few targets, everyone else was missing a whole lot more than he was. It also taught him to bring hand warmers to cold events.

- Finding out the impact of dehydration on her vision, an athlete placed her water bottle in a readily accessible place and took frequent sips.

These are competition-related problems you can only learn to deal with and correct after competition-related experiments. The only way to find out these real competition situations is to put yourself on the line, make mistakes and figure it out (iGPS!). And when you do, there's no need for disappointment ever again. Instead, pat yourself on the back for putting yourself on the line and for learning so much about this great experiment of competing with your peers.

2. **Learning from the best.** You get to hang around and watch champions who are better than you, so you can copy and learn from them. As a coach, I remember my youngest karate students playing tag in the bleachers at a competition, and somehow they still always came back from competitions having learned an astounding amount, just by being around top competitors.

   In chapter 12, I'll talk about how hanging around top performers makes learning easy and natural. Plus, your parents get to hang around other parents and observe and learn how to do and not do competition support. (It is all a big experiment for them, too.)

3. **It's fun.** Hey, you get to go away for a weekend or longer and see all of your friends. That's fun. And your parents get

to watch you gain more experience and grow. That's really important, because they grow too.

4. **Responsibility.** You learn proper sportsmanship, safety and citizenship. Who would ever have thought a competition was like a science experiment and could deliver this? Well you know now.

Be a scientist. Experimenting with competition is necessary to build your competition skills. You will make mistakes, and trust me, you will figure it out. It is the key thing you must do in order to become a champion. *And, as your parents need to know all of this, as well, you can leave your book open on this page on the kitchen table.*

Skill Drill 8: Losing makes you stronger

You will become the expert experimenter in competing *by competing*—sometimes by getting angry, frustrated and disappointed. But you'll use this iGPS to guide you. And you'll treat all of your mistakes (and resulting emotions) as the necessary pain for learning how to become a champion.

AND, might I add, it'll improve your relationship with your parents, as you and they will be on the same page of becoming a winning team (which we'll get to in a later chapter)! And, hey, you might even appreciate your science classes more.

Next up

In the next chapter, we'll enter Step 4 and add the third and final component of your operating system. You will start the process of fixing the pain of your iGPS disasters with a whole new set of tools we'll start calling iAPPs, and, remarkably, it may be painless.

Training Tip

Talk to your parents about when you want to discuss your game and when you don't want to. Perhaps set a plan where you stay quietly in your Zone at the start with no talking distractions, while you ramp up for your competition.

Then, when the competition is finished, you can set a cooling down period of a couple of hours while you take the off ramp. And then you can talk. Or not. But let everyone know your plan beforehand.

" *It [the Zone] is like meditation. You must find your inner peace and focus on your goal.*

— JESSICA ROSSI,
Star Skeet Shooter "

TEEN vs TARGET PLAYBOOK

STEP 4

INSTALL AND APPLY
THE TOOLS OF CHAMPIONS

This is the third part of your operating system. You know your goal is to win. You've identified the GPS that is messing you up. Now you'll learn the applications (iAPPs) to fix the stuff that causes you to fail. No emotions. No tears. Get the job done.

> *"When I step onto the court, I don't have to think about anything. If I have a problem off the court, I find that after I play, my mind is clearer and I can come up with a better solution. It's like therapy. It relaxes me and allows me to solve problems.*

— **MICHAEL JORDAN**
Star Basketball Player

9
BE A TECH

Apply your toolkit to reboot your game.

> *To uncover your true potential you must first find your own limits and then you have to have the courage to blow past them.*
>
> **— PICABO STREET,**
> Star Skier

In the previous chapter, I suggested that the only way for you to win is to get out there and put yourself on the line and experiment with your game, as failing gives you the opportunity to fix your mistakes and continually improve.

Although mistakes really hurt, and sometimes result in teary eyes, hulls whipped forcibly into bins and lots of barely audible muttering at one's stupidity, they reveal your passion. And you will need every bit of that passion in order to become a champion. But please keep your outbursts short and invisible to others, as you are now going to learn the tools to channel that passion into winning.

So where does passion leave you? Well, in Step 4, which is the most exciting part, wouldn't you know? That of rebooting your game, just like you might reboot your phone. Although treating your mind like a cell phone and shutting it down and starting it up again is impossible, in the next chapters you'll be learning several very useful ways of rebooting your game when it fails you.

When your skills are lagging and it is as though your learning speed wheel shows "loading…" and just spins and spins and spins, you are going to learn to be a TECH (technician), with the passion, skills and the proper tools to fix your game.

Your mind needs more than just better broadband and increased upload and download speeds. It needs "rebooting" strategies to deal with all manner of problems. We'll call these strategies iAPPs (internal applications) and you'll use them just like you might use the applications on your cell phone.

You need strategies that work

Believe it or not, you already have several internal applications. Of course, some of them may or may not work. Like throwing shells and muttering bad words under your breath at yourself.

These actions are really an attempt to change things up and get yourself angry, in order to get your adrenaline ramped up. And it

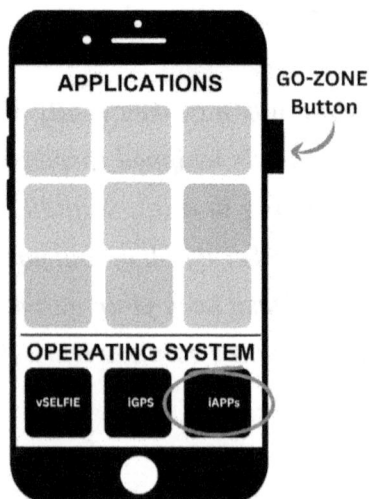

APPLICATIONS

GO-ZONE Button

OPERATING SYSTEM

vSELFIE   iGPS   iAPPs

sometimes works—and it more often doesn't. And then, similar to your screen freezing, your game goes into what is called the *death spiral* and the empty hulls really start flying.

The act of *blaming* is another internal application and sometimes it works to make you feel a little better. Like blaming the weather. That works to take the pressure off you, because the heat or rain or wind can really affect your game.

But you haven't learned much about how to perform in heat or rain or wind when you blame the weather. And the next competition with heat or rain or wind may see you missing just as many targets and in just as much emotional pain.

Blaming distracting people is another, such as miss-prone squadmates, grumpy officials, upset parents or concerned coaches. But you haven't learned much about how to deal with people when you blame them. And the next time…

Blaming poorly-thrown targets, bad backgrounds or poorly-lit targets are three more. And again, by blaming these things, you haven't learned much about how to deal with obstacles in your game. And the next time…

New strategies to build success

So, instead of these awkward attempts to deal with your failures with applications that only work some of the time, in this part of the book you are going to learn applications that do work—most of the time. And this is where your role as TECH comes in. It will require that you step back, metaphorically pop open the casing on your brain, examine the messiness of your actions and thinking and insert an iAPP. Here's what you'll learn:

- **Rather than throw shells in an attempt to build up your adrenaline,** you are going to learn an iAPP that will allow you to build adrenaline easily and naturally.
- **Rather than blame people, you are going to learn an iAPP to bring people down to size** and, in some cases, make them "disappear" so that you can focus entirely on the target—not them.
- **Rather than blame the weather, you are going to learn an iAPP to change rain to sun, calm the wind and cool the heat.** Sounds impossible, doesn't it? And if it sounds like magic, then welcome to the magical power of your mind.
- **Rather than blame the trap machines or the range, you are going to learn an iAPP to make the targets look impressively large and slow.** It too sounds impossible. But welcome again to the power of what champions do all of the time.

Skill Drill 9: TECH-time

So, put on your coveralls, Mr. or Ms. TECH, and get ready to get messy. Because we are going to pop open the hood on your high-performance machine and start to make major adjustments with a whole new set of iAPPS.

To prepare for your new role as TECH, you must work very hard at staying in your GO-ZONE. But as you'll fall out of it at times, I suggest that you make a list of all the competition situations that cause you to lose it, and that can include school stuff as well.

These are the things that you, the TECH, want to repair, and will soon be repairing so you'll be able to stay in the GO-ZONE in your next competition. We'll refer to these situations as the NO-ZONE, and sometimes they hurt and result in tears. The following chart has some examples of the NO-ZONE.

EXAMPLES OF A NO-ZONE LIST

- My older sibling/friend beats me all the time in clays and I get angry
- I lose one target and then drop three more
- I was told not to think of score but people are mean and tell me my score
- The wind really makes me careful and I miss
- I feel out of shape and get tired at long competitions, but I hate fitness stuff
- I get mad and throw things
- My school GPA is lousy and I need to get all A's, but school is boring
- I fear shoot-offs (but I've never been in one)
- I get sleepy after a big lunch

In review:

- **Keep upleveling your game** by using your GO-ZONE as your green light, go-for-it signal.
- **Keep playing your adrenalized *v*SELFIE** to overcome your nervousness in your game (and your presentations at school).
- **Make your list of all the iGPS NO-ZONE situations that pull you out of your GO-ZONE.**

To get started, pull out your coveralls and be prepared for a momentary change of career, that of being your own clays-game TECH. Because high-level competition requires that you troubleshoot your game, repair what's not working and put together some successes.

Next up

In the next chapter, you'll be adding a powerful and useful iAPP to your game and to your role as TECH. You'll be learning how to forget those awful times in competitions where you felt bad and never got out of that NO-ZONE feeling. You are going to learn to forget those kinds of competitions and treat them as though they never happened. And it's pretty awesome actually, because forgetting that kind of stuff feels really good.

Training Tip

Keep a running list of the iGPS stuff that pulls you out of your GO-ZONE. Perhaps by now you have found a journal to keep track of them and cross them off as you fix them. Perhaps you are using a cell phone app to keep track of them.

The reason I like keeping this list is that I get great pleasure crossing off the problems I've fixed. And then I celebrate, as it shows my progress.

As well, you might put your NO-ZONE list in an envelope along with your goals list that you prepared in Skill Drill 1, Chapter 1.

Address the letter to yourself and mail the letter at the post office. When you receive it, place it in a safe place until the end of the season and then open it and see how many goals have been achieved and how many blocks have been resolved.

"

*I figure practice puts your brains
in your muscles.*

— SAM SNEAD,
STAR GOLFER

"

10
LEARN TO FORGET

Erase past game mistakes and frustrations.

> " *What to do with a mistake: recognize it,*
> *admit it, learn from it, forget it.*
>
> **— DEAN SMITH,**
> STAR COACH "

The time has arrived. Welcome to TECH school. It is time to repair the NO-ZONE problems that are causing you to feel bad and miss targets. In the last chapter I asked you to make a list of what you want to fix. If you haven't done it yet, please do it now so we can have fun tinkering.

When was the last time a teacher sat you down and said, "Okay, class, today we are going to learn how to forget?" Like, sure, a teacher is *not* going to say something like that. Forget the date of your nation's birthday? Forget the radius of a circle? Forget multiplication? Forget how to spell "graduation?"

It may not be good to forget *some* stuff. But what about those five dropped targets in a row last year that caused you to lose the championship, and it is still bothering you? What about being teased after losing? What about your parents getting mad at you for throwing shells? Forgetting that kind of stuff would be okay. Right?

Well, believe it or not, we are already pretty good at forgetting without any new iAPP. I'm sure that you have studied for a test or exam and the next day you forgot some part of what you studied. Right? That is frustrating, but it happens.

Forgetting is actually a very good skill! Maybe not for history or calculus or chemistry or any other school subject. But missing the last four clays and the resulting embarrassment—absolutely!

Unfortunately, sometimes it takes months, weeks and decades to let go of a memory, like the death of my much-loved family pet, Lacey. But when I got a new puppy, Hailey, my joy for Hailey was pretty intense and in a week or two my brain pushed aside the sad memory of Lacey's passing.

In most of your life, that kind of forgetting works pretty well and is normal. But in competitive sports, it's difficult waiting for your clays game to be kinder to you with more wins. Nor can you imagine going to a competition where everyone lets you win just to help you forget your losing past. So, as it won't happen automatically, you'll have to learn an iAPP to take charge of forgetting all by yourself.

And that is just what you'll do here. For you to become a champion, all those misses need to be pushed aside by good memories of the times you positively smoked targets, and here is where you become the TECH.

Skill Drill 10: Learn to forget mistakes

Forgetting is normal, and you just have to speed it up a bit. Instead of it taking months or years of successful competitions to forget the unsuccessful ones, you'll make it as instantaneous as a snap of your fingers with the SNAP iAPP.

It is a bit like using the pleasant scent of an air freshener to eliminate foul smells. I won't explain exactly how it works except to say it gets good memories to eliminate bad memories. And trust me, it typically results in a lovely fragrance.

1. **Think of a mistake you really *need* to forget, like a time you fell apart in a competition**. Notice how the memory may make you angry and tense up, also called the NO-ZONE. As you are thinking of that memory, pinch (press) your *left* thumb and index fingers together for several seconds, then release them. The pinch has captured the memory of the NO-ZONE problem, like capturing the unpleasant smell of old smelly cheese.

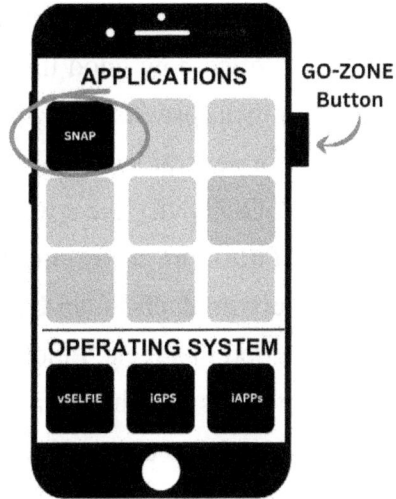

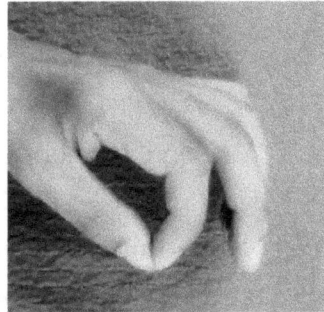

2. **Now think of a GO-ZONE memory where you crushed clays and had a fantastic round or part of a round.** Notice how good this feels. Switch hands this time, and pinch (press) your *right* thumb and index fingers together for several seconds, then release. You have captured the GO-ZONE, like a wonderful scent of hot chocolate!

3. **Think of a second GO-ZONE memory where you crushed clays and had a fantastic time.** Notice how good this feels. Pinch (press) your *right* thumb and index fingers together, again, for several seconds, then release. You have captured another GO-ZONE, like the pleasant scent of popcorn!

4. **Think of a third GO-ZONE memory where you crushed clays and had a fantastic time.** Notice how good this feels. Pinch (press) your *right* thumb and index fingers together, again, for several seconds, then release. You have captured yet another GO-ZONE, and the pleasant smells of hamburgers on the grill! These GO-ZONE memories have started to add up!

5. **Now, be a TECH and apply (press) both *right* and *left* finger pinches together at the same time.** This is where you combine the GO-ZONE and the NO-ZONE memories, and in a snap, the three GO-ZONE memories gang up on the NO-ZONE one, similar to how well your three food scents might block out the foul scent of smelly cheese.

6. **Finally, after holding the pinches for several seconds, check your memory of the NO-ZONE event and see if you can still remember it.** If you've forgotten it already, yay! If not, repeat the SNAP iAPP until it smells good. I mean, until it feels GO-ZONE good! Remarkably, forgetting like this can really be as quick as a snap.

Practice playing TECH and repair other memories and other stinky parts of your game with SNAP. But there is one more thing you need to know. Your brain is on your side. Every time you miss and deal with the resulting anger or frustration of missing, by using SNAP, your brain gets better at figuring out how to stay in the GO-ZONE and win in clays.

Through SNAP and other iAPPs, you are educating your brain. You miss; you get angry; you fix it with SNAP; and your brain learns. And everything smells better in the long run. The more you use the SNAP iAPP, eventually it will work for you automatically to eliminate NO-ZONE memories, so you'll be effortlessly smoking targets like a champion. And, as one of my athletes told me, "It'll give you the memory of a goldfish," and help you to let go of NO-ZONE memories really fast!

Next up

In the next chapter, I'll take you through SNAP again. This time, you'll use it to deal with your pre-competition or pre-exam nerves. In the meantime, remember to stay in your GO-ZONE, create nerves-free competitions with your vSELFIE and resolve iGPS mistakes with SNAP. Be the TECH.

Training Tip

When you are competing or practicing (or trying to stay focused at school) and a NO-ZONE distraction pops into your mind, think of it as a fly zipping by.

Quickly imagine catching it securely between your thumb and index fingers (*left-hand* pinch) and then think of and capture three GO-ZONE memories with your other hand (*right-hand* pinch).

Then crush the thought by pinching both simultaneously. As quick as a snap, your SNAP iAPP removes the distracting thought and your focus returns. Here's the challenge. See how many NO-ZONES you can fix in an hour, day or week.

11
BANISH NERVES

Harness the joy of competing.

Wow, you have come a long way. A thousand miles (1609.34 km)!
You've now got your GO-ZONE happy place. You've got your
operating system, with vSELFIE, iGPS and iAPPs. And now you
can be the TECH with your first iAPP—SNAP.

In the last chapter, I promised one more use for SNAP, and that was
for getting ready for a competition or an exam in school. But first, a
quick note on why SNAP works so well. Physiology! That's right.
Your posture and everything that goes with it. Physiology is your
posture, your breathing—everything both internal and external in
and on your body. Skin perspiration is physiology. Shivering is
physiology.

When you are in the NO-ZONE, your physiology is down-
leveled, such as with a defeated posture where you are slouched,

tense, disconnected, awkward and fatigued.

When you are in the GO-ZONE, your physiology is upleveled, such as being upright, powerful, relaxed, intense (rather than tense) and coordinated with fabulous visual acuity. Good physiology is so important!

When you use SNAP with the *left* pinch for the NO-ZONE memory (down-leveled physiology) and three *right* pinches for the GO-ZONE memories (up-leveled physiology), AND then pinch both pinches at the same time, your brain tries to sort out which physiology to keep. I can imagine which physiology *you* want to keep—the up-leveled one that will crush more clays— and, unsurprisingly, so does your brain.

As you can imagine, your brain is very smart and happy with that choice, as up-leveled physiology is stronger and moves better to the target and just feels good. So your brain sloshes between the two and selects the up-leveled one.

Simple.
That is how the SNAP iAPP uses physiology
to help you to succeed in your game.

Fixing nervousness

Now, in your role as TECH, there is a lot of stuff you want to fix— like fear before a competition. Some people think being fearful and nervous is normal. I used to.

Well, it is not.

Some people think we just have to accept it and learn to live with it.

No, we do not.

In your game, whether it's to win a local competition or a national or world-class event, embracing nervousness or fear is total nonsense. You need to take control and make being in your GO-ZONE normal and fun in your competitions.

Case in point

I was working with a young runner who struggled with her main event, the 400-metre run. She was always very nervous at the start, because she knew what awaited her at the 200-metre mark. Halfway through, she would hit a wall.

I asked her to think back to a recent event where that wall blocked her success, and her face immediately contorted as though in pain. Up to that point in my training career, I'd never witnessed such pain in someone's "normal" mental block.

"Use SNAP," I yelled, startling her. "Pinch your *left* hand."

She immediately did and I followed it up.

> **"Quickly, now think of a GO-ZONE
> experience and pinch your *right*."**

She pressed her fingers together.

> **"And another," I said. "And the last one."**

She did.

> **"And now pinch them both."**

She did and immediately smiled.

This was SNAP in a crisis, but we also applied it to other *normally stressful* parts of her race, so she could enjoy setting the pace, respond quickly to someone challenging her and enjoy the final sprint to the tape. Needless to say, her next event was spectacular. Embrace nervousness? Are you kidding me? She learned to resolve her nerves instead.

Skill Drill 11: SNAP for competition preparation

Now here is the SNAP iAPP again (and again and again). In this practice, use it to develop joyful anticipation for your next competition:

1. **Pinch your *left-hand* finger pinch to capture the feeling of anxiety** (the down-leveled physiology).
2. **Think of a fabulous time when you perfectly crushed targets and pinch your *right-hand* finger pinch to capture that GO-ZONE** (the up-leveled physiology of success). You now know the process. Do this step twice more, with other (adrenalized) GO-ZONE events.

3. **Finally, press both pinches at the same time (SNAP)** and notice how your brain molds the memories into a wonderful feeling with a physiology that is ready to compete. (Tip: do it over and over until you get the result you want.)

   With your SNAP iAPP, develop the feeling of euphoria for competing. And when you combine SNAP with your vSELFIE, you will truly be on the prowl for a championship.

One more extra little tip:

If you feel a little edgy at the start of your competition
(formerly called nerves)
reframe this feeling as your body simply getting ready.

Use your SNAP iAPP to improve other potentially stressful areas of your life. How excited can you get for writing an exam? For writing SATs? For sitting for your driver's license exam? For the next few weeks use SNAP frequently, and get it to work for you subconsciously. With practice, a NO-ZONE memory of a missed target or problem will be gone in an instant, probably before you can even think of using your iAPP.

Next up

As you continue to fix your game and play the role of TECH, keep in mind that SNAP is the normal way our minds deal with memories that we want to forget or want to override, like that former feeling of nervousness before a competition. You are simply upleveling your game physiology that will allow you to stay in your GO-ZONE and be consistent.

In the next chapter, we'll take this up-leveling physiology to a whole new level with an iAPP that will allow you to copy the skills of top athletes really fast—like really, really, really fast.

Training Tip

Force yourself to think of situations that make you nervous, such as imagining yourself in your vSELFIE in a world-class event. You are on the screen going head to head with some of the best clays' athletes in the world.

If you feel a hint of nervousness, use SNAP to resolve it. Put yourself in shoot-offs or other nerve-wracking situations and use SNAP over and over to resolve any nervousness.

Finally, use SNAP during car and plane travel to competitions. When you get there, you'll be in your GO-ZONE and unstoppable.

12
MODEL YOUR HEROES

Integrate their skills into your game.

> "
>
> *We need role models*
> *who are going to break the mold.*
>
> **— CARLY SIMON,**
> STAR SINGER AND SONGWRITER
>
> "

Onward and upward with becoming a champion. Your GO-ZONE. Your vSELFIE. Your iGPS. And being a TECH with your SNAP iAPP. You have developed your operating system for excellence and are well on your way to learning how to win championships.

I wish I'd had these tools when I was your age. But it's no time to get sentimental, as I have a brand-new iAPP to teach you and it is one of my favorites.

It was 20 years ago that one of the world's best Olympians at clays transformed the game of skeet. Most top Olympians in International Skeet were "old" guys in their 30s and 40s before they ever got close to winning.

But the current world's GOAT (Greatest Of All Time) was only 16 years old when he won his first World Cup. And most athletes would be content with that, except in the same year he also reached the podium in four other events. He has now won four Olympic gold medals, and he is still going strong.

His name is Vincent Hancock and in Paris 2024 he once again won gold. For those of you who are 16 years of age or younger, this might just blow your mind. I mean, could you win an Olympic medal right now? What would it take? Train a lot? Be a gifted athlete? Have great coaches? All of the above, of course, but there's something more and very basic. And that is in your knack for learning quickly.

The science of learning

I'll give it to you full blast! In addition to an athlete's coaches, training and athletic abilities, top athletes have something that you also have—mirror neurons. Mirror neurons are what I call "copycat" neurons or "monkey-see, monkey-do" neurons.

Or "mimic" neurons. You have them too. Science tells us that our brain's grey matter is chalk full of these neurons. Let's learn to use them to our advantage.

Some neurons store information, some neurons transmit information from brain region to brain region and other neurons are designed to learn. See it; do it.

The learning neuron—mirror neurons—have an amazing copycat ability that is automatic and gives you an exact copy of another person's muscle movements, breathing, moving to the target and even facial expressions. Mirror neurons are how you learned almost everything you do, from hitting your target to learning how to speak. Learning is instantaneous. In the "blink of the eye" fast.

Think of a time when your friend yawned and you did too. Or you scratched your head and she did too. That is mirror neurons at play. They connect us to people. They are a part of empathy and sympathy, as when we see someone crying we may cry too. (Not me, of course!) But in learning a skill like clays, they help us to learn all manner of mounts, moves to the target and reactions to our competitors. Fast! Just like gold-medal Olympians.

Skill Drill 12: Using mirror neurons to model your heroes

Now let's be a TECH again. The following exercise can help you to instantly copy the world-class performers you see at competitions and fix some weakness in your game. And, if you are lucky, you may have these champions at your home club. However, if you like to stay at home, then you can fire up your cell phone and watch them (and copy them) on YouTube (with your parents permission, of course).

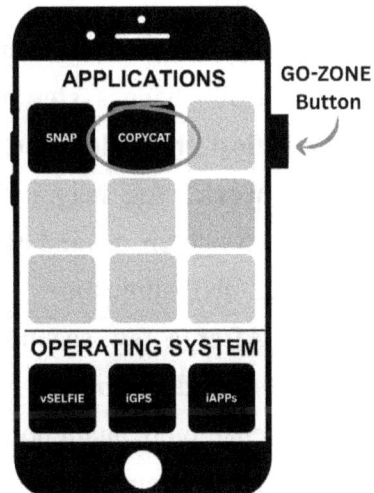

1. **Think of a skill you'd like (need) to get better at.** Now imagine your image on your vSELFIE in a specific, intense part of your competition where that skill is absolutely needed. Notice that you may be in the NO-ZONE and having a difficult time.

2. **Next, think of three champions in your sport.** Imagine all three champions standing beside you on your left.

3. **Now you are going to step to your left and step into the imagined shoes of these champions**. This will trigger your mirror neurons, allowing you to learn multiple new and wonderful things from these champions, such as new shooting skills, new ways of processing the speed of objects, greater peripheral awareness, faster reflexes, new perceptional ability to slow objects down and on and on and on.

   If you are ready for these kinds of wonderful champion-level changes, **step over into the imagined shoes of the first champion and let your mirror neurons do their work.** You may (will) feel your posture (physiology) straighten up and you may (will) feel a burst of GO-ZONE adrenaline.

4. **After a few seconds, step again into the shoes of a second champion.** And then step into the shoes of a third champion, again noticing the new GO-ZONE feelings of connecting with them via your mirror neurons. You may feel way more confident and, hey, that is what mirror neurons do.

They typically give you the sense that you can do what the champions do, immediately, because you are copying both their skillful physiology and GO-ZONE posture, as well as the feeling that goes with it.

5. **Now, bring the imagined image of yourself back from your *v*SELFIE** and teach that *you* what you just learned from the three champions.

6. **Then, imagine stepping into the stand.** If that feels good, great! Call pull, pull the trigger and smoke it. If it could feel even better, redo the exercise until it does. And then go test out your new skill(s) on the range.

As you can imagine, being the TECH and using the COPYCAT iAPP gives you a huge advantage in the learning department in everything you do. Even in school where you are typically discouraged from trying to copy your classmates, this kind of copying is totally different and totally legal.

It is way too much fun as a fast way of learning, and, instead of trying to stop you, teachers will encourage you to do it, especially when they see how fast you learn. It is normal to learn this way, because our brain's mirror neurons are wired to do it.

Now, while you are at the range, if anything gets you frustrated, be the TECH and COPYCAT some champions. If any skill seems difficult, COPYCAT some champions. If math or science or chemistry gets you down at school, COPYCAT teachers or your parents or that genius aunt of yours. Oh, one last thing. Using COPYCAT is a great way to get you back in your GO-ZONE in almost any area of your life.

Next up

With your new expertise as a TECH and this book as a guide, stay in your GO-ZONE by using your iAPPS of COPYCAT and SNAP and start to repair your game problems. In the next chapter, we'll look at shielding your mirror neurons to prevent them from copying wrong behaviors from others, such as nervousness or anger or sadness or bad technique. Because protecting your mirror neurons matters a lot, as they are the main cause of competition failures in the way they vacuum up all manner of bad skills and behaviors.

Training Tip

After you have finished your next competition, go to the grandstand or shoot-off area and watch the top athletes go toe to toe with each other.

Pick your favorite athlete (role model) and in the back where nobody can see you, pretend to be that athlete.

Step into the stand like they do, adjust and prepare like they do and pretend to mount and move to the target like they do. Repeat this process for the whole round.

When the round is finished, notice how good and empowered you feel. And then be thankful you have mirror neurons.

13
PROTECT YOUR FOCUS

Activate Bob's 30-Minute Rule before competing.

You are well on your way to success. You've got your GO-ZONE to start your system. Your operating system of vSELFIE for the brilliant image of success that you want, your iGPS for guidance to keep you on track and your iAPPs of SNAP and COPYCAT for midcourse corrections.

Find at least five minutes each day to practice and apply these to your game. As well, use your new iAPPS in school and for your other activities. Now, we'll look at learning the wrong stuff and how to make it right.

When I was 14 years old, I learned to play golf with rented clubs, regular gym shoes and no lessons, and within a month I played exceptionally well on our local golf course. I scored better then than I can do now, even with way more practice, more expensive clubs and all the right accessories. I was a natural back then, I thought, until I learned about mirror neurons and found that they'd helped me copy the pros I'd seen on TV in a very real monkey-see, monkey-do process.

I even noticed way back then that my hockey team played better against a strong team than we did against a weaker team. I now know that our mirror neurons copied the strong team's GO-ZONE and skill, and then, with the weaker team, we copied their NO-ZONE and lack of skill. While copying the strong team gave us an unexpected boost, copying the weak team bogged us down. Interesting?

Mirror neurons are designed to copy, and they are exceptionally good at it. They never think about good or bad form or GO-ZONE or NO-ZONE—they just copy. And when you find yourself copying lousy form or nervousness or tiredness, you are copying the wrong people.

I call this very natural process of copying the wrong people the *copycat blues*. And that is where you come in. You have to copy only the best, and stop copying the rest. (I like that rhyme.)

With the COPYCAT iAPP, you specifically learned how to copy the best, by stepping into the shoes of champions and triggering your mirror neurons to copy their physiology (and skills).

But you have to protect your mirror neurons from unskillful competitors, blocking them out much like those little black horse blinders on the sides of a horse's head protects the horse from distractions. Because your mirror neurons are really prone to vacuuming up poor skills and bad behaviors and making them your own!

One of my more skillful karate students would go to competitions and be the best friend of all the other competitors in his category. He'd be chatting and joking with them right up to the start of his first round. And then he'd make silly mistakes in competition and act like he'd lost all of his skill. He had to learn the hard way that he was opening up his mirror neurons to copy them and that made him very vulnerable.

So, like him, if you are chatting with your Best Friend (BF) before a competition and your BF is not very skillful—you'll be copying their lack of skill. And if they are nervous, you'll be copying their nervousness. And if they are frustrated, you'll be copying their frustration. That is right! That is how well these mirror neurons work when it comes to learning, and that means every human behavior whether you want to copy it or not! And it definitely creates the copycat blues.

Skill Drill 14: Bob's 30-Minute Rule (30MR)

Locking yourself in a padded room is not the answer, but there is one way to protect your mirror neurons, and that is by using my 30-Minute Rule (30MR):

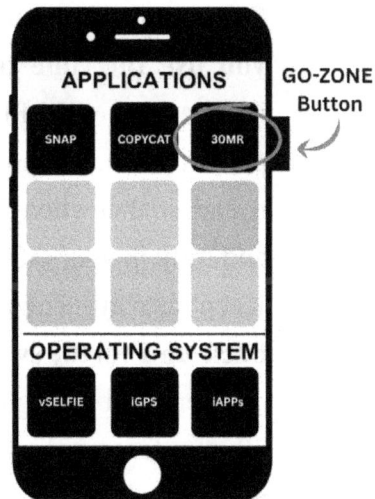

APPLICATIONS

GO-ZONE Button

SNAP   COPYCAT   30MR

OPERATING SYSTEM

vSELFIE   iGPS   iAPPs

1. **Before each competition, start your preparation a full 30 or more minutes before your round begins by getting away from everyone.** And that means everyone. No parents, coaches, teammates or opponents.

   This is you putting up imaginary horse blinders to protect your mirror neurons. This may seem odd, as one of the reasons you play sports is to meet and make new friends, but it is based on 30 years of working with athletes like you. By keeping your distance, your game will uplevel exponentially.

   Some of my athletes enlist their parents or coaches to block friends, fellow athletes and other distracting individuals from going anywhere near them. Most importantly, all of my athletes turn off their cell phones to stop that vulnerable access point. With the 30MR, you ignore people, and if necessary, apologize later—after you win. You can blame me (Bob) for making you do it.

2. **During this 30-minute period when you isolate yourself, you use the time to get into your GO-ZONE.** Feel it! Use your vSELFIE to watch yourself crushing clays perfectly. Then vSELFIE at least one great, adrenalized round, so that when the first round starts, you are pumped and fully in your GO-ZONE groove.

3. **Keep moving during the whole 30 minutes, pacing back and forth,** swaying back and forth. In upcoming chapters, I'll give you more iAPPS to use during this 30-minute period of getting ready. But for now, keep moving and be sure to keep your eyes at the horizon, as

looking at the ground can be a big GO-ZONE buster. And if people get in your way, look right through them. If they want to talk, point to your earbuds and shrug, even if you aren't listening to music. Or tell them to go away and blame Bob!

And that is Bob's 30MR. It's a rule you must live by if you wish to stay focused and win a championship. Putting up horse blinders protects your distractible mirror neurons. Mirror neurons are beautiful learning devices, but you must ensure that they are learning the right skills from the right people at the right time.

Next up

In the next chapter we take our strategies to the classroom in order to get your homework done faster so that you'll have more time to practice clays and socialize. And both can be really fun.

Place two chairs facing each other and sit face to face with a friend. First, try to get your friend to smile, where your friend tries to keep a straight face and ignore your antics.

Training Tip

And then have your friend try to get you to smile, while you keep a straight face. Notice how difficult it is to keep from smiling.

Typically, because of mirror neurons, it is very easy for another person to get us to smile. More interestingly, it is just as easy for another person to get us to be nervous or skill-less too! And this exercise demonstrates why your 30MR is so important.

14
BE A WILDFIRE

*Spread your passion beyond sport
to school and life.*

"

*Knowledge is power, and school is where you
start to gain your superpowers.*

— UNKNOWN,
STAR EDUCATOR

"

*You have come so far in the book! The Zone. Your operating
system of vSELFIE, internal feedback with iGPS and your
iAPPs with the multiple applications of SNAP, COPYCAT and
30MR.*

*Take a break from reading, practice and apply these iAPPs to
your game, as they don't work, you do. And if you are in school,
as you likely are, apply your iAPPs to your non-clays activities
and your personal life. In this chapter, we'll look at why doing
well in school is tied to how well you do in your game.*

I had an eye-popping experience recently. One of my adult
champions in American Skeet told me that because of my clinic,

several years ago when he was a teenager, he never ever had to take notes in college or even crack open a textbook.

And it was not because he was lazy. Rather, it was because dyslexia hampered his taking notes by distracting and frustrating him, and so did studying from them afterwards. But with the same iAPPs that you are learning in this program, he was able to overcome his dyslexic note-taking problem!

First, he always sat at the front of the room, right in front of his professor, so there would be fewer distractions. He used his GO-ZONE to stay focused. And, most importantly, he used his COPYCAT iAPP to model everything about his professors—the way they moved, made hand gestures, expressed emotions and he then mentally processed their expertise.

His mirror neurons were literally immersed in the professors' way of thinking. And, in this manner, he told me he could remember everything a professor said in the lecture, and simply "filled in the blanks" during exams.

As this kind of success has been repeated time and again by my other athletes, I should not have been surprised, but I am always delighted to hear success in school, as it also means success on the range. These iAPPs are powerful stuff.

School as practice for winning and vice versa

So why, in a clays high-performance playbook, would I talk about school? Well, four reasons:

1. **Do well in school, do well in competition.** I've found that when my athletes are doing well in school, it is a good

indicator that they are also doing well in clays training and competition. Because this program creates resiliency, and that becomes the normal way to approach everything you do in life.

2. **More time for clays practice.** When my clays athletes are doing well in school, they are way more efficient and typically get their homework done faster and then have more time to spend on clays practice and other things.

3. **Ideal place to practice your GO-ZONE, vSELFIE and iAPPS.** School is a great place to practice the iAPPs you are learning in this book, so you can better apply them to winning in clays.

   In school you face lots of challenges with new subjects, organizing your thoughts on essays and learning how to present orally to and communicate with your peers and adults. The number of blocks you encounter can be far greater than in your sport. So think of school as practice for winning.

4. **This program and the iAPPs cannot be contained to just sport.** It is important for you and your parents to know that these iAPPs have applications that spread beyond your sport, where they benefit your abilities as a leader, a good friend and a good citizen. As you will find as you move deeper into this book, you will start to wear your Zone on your sleeve. People will notice. It is contagious.

Skill Drill 14: Apply your GO-ZONE to school

Here are a couple of examples of using iAPPs to eliminate frustration, the kind you might get in class when you fail to understand a question on a history, math, physics, chemistry or English exam (or all of the above).

1. **You struggle with a question on your history exam.** The answer is on the tip of your tongue, but you're frustrated. You remember SNAP and pinch your *left* thumb and index fingers together. And then you pinch three GO-ZONE experiences on the *right* hand and then finish it. The frustration disappears and you answer the question and dive into the next one.

2. **You struggle to remember a mathematics equation.** To break through your frustration, you think that COPYCAT might help you. You imagine your teacher and two math whizzes squeezed beside you on your exam chair. You then imagine moving into their shoes. After a few seconds, your frustration disappears. You smile, move on to the question and finish the exam, and then back to the one you found difficult.

3. **You struggle getting ready for a presentation.** You use the COPYCAT iAPP to model your favorite teachers. You use the SNAP iAPP to override your fear of presenting by accepting that presenting is fun and no different than speaking to your family or friends. You fire up your vSELFIE with lots of adrenaline and watch it over and over. After several crazy sessions with your vSELFIE, it feels like it will go just fine.

Similar to these examples, apply your iAPPs to all aspects of your academic life. You may not be able to forgo writing notes in class like my other athlete did, and you'll probably have to open your textbook and read a few chapters to study, but all in all, your grades can only improve.

Plus, with a better handle on your schooling, you'll have way more time to practice the sport you love. And pretty soon, iAPPs will become embedded in how you think about everything, especially your quest for a championship.

Next up

In the next chapter, get ready to see the targets as big, bright and slow as you will soon have an iAPP to do that. And hey, you may even start to perform well enough to get a scholarship at a reputable college.

Training Tip

Do the following experiment during school. Get into your GO-ZONE in a class and stay in it for a whole class. Notice how much different it feels and how much better you might be focusing and understanding the material.

And especially notice how the teacher might be treating you a bit differently. Then notice how much more information you retain with way less studying.

"

The more difficult the victory,
the greater the happiness in winning.

— PELÉ,
STAR SOCCER PLAYER

"

15
IMPROVE VISUAL ACUITY

Magnify and slow down targets.

"

*If you can believe it,
the mind can achieve it.*

— RONNIE LOTT,
STAR FOOTBALL PLAYER

"

Wow, do you ever have a great toolkit, now. And, who would have guessed that you can use this toolkit for becoming a better student along with being a better athlete. Several of my past teenage athletes have even gone on to become great coaches and business leaders, too. Dream big and practice smart.

A number of years ago, I competed at my karate national championships. It was the biggest event of my karate life and to this day, I can still "see" the crowds of excited competitors lined up in rows on the shining hardwood floors.

My memories are filled with images that are big and bright. Clear as crystal. Lots of excited competitors close around me. Everything is in brilliant technicolor. It was a very hyperaware and focused experience, and when I revisit that memory, it produces an immediate exhilarating feeling in my core. GO-ZONE all the way!

But… a year later, the next tournament was a totally different story—180 degrees different. The registration dragged on into the morning because of long lines of unexpected competitors. As a result, my competition was pushed back to late afternoon/evening and was moved to a student cafeteria, as the main complex had to be made ready for a concert that evening.

The cold, vinyl covered floors of the cafeteria quickly developed a slippery sheen from the humidity caused by the breathing of the athletes. Footing was a little treacherous. The lighting was dimmer, casting shadows over the ring. My opponents kind of seemed bigger and louder and more threatening. My lower back tightened up. A troubling NO-ZONE feeling weighed down my core.

I closed my eyes and gave my head a prolonged shake and in a moment of clarity, I accessed the previous year's memory. The big, bright, clear experience of me winning, and the GO-ZONE feeling in my core as a medal was put over my head and onto my shoulders.

- Bright image
- Sharp image
- Colorful image

My name was soon to be called. In a desperate move, I physically reached my hands out in front of me and imagined grabbing the previous year's brilliant, bright and colorful image like a sheet of wallpaper. Quickly, I plastered it over the current and awful NO-ZONE image of the cafeteria.

With a flurry of hand gestures that probably resembled a weird karate form, I frantically stretched the NO-ZONE image to make it look like the GO-ZONE one. In those dynamic seconds, in my mind, I repeatedly inserted:

Bright in place of dark.
Sharp in place of fuzzy.
Color in place of shadow.
And clarity of me on the podium
in place of a myriad of dark images.

Instantly, like really instantly, I was flush with the GO-ZONE again. Exhilaration! Adrenaline! Power! My mind was clear with zero thinking. Ten-feet tall—I was ten-feet tall and my opponents were ants!

My name was called, and I entered the ring. Frankly, I don't remember any of my matches after that, except that I have the first-place trophy to show for it.

See targets differently

Believe it or not, your brain records and retrieves memories the same way mine does. Sometimes bright; sometimes dark. Sometimes sharp; sometimes fuzzy. Sometimes in color; sometimes in black and white.

And it all depends on how good or bad the memory of the event felt. And now that you know this, it gives you the leverage to make huge changes in your game where you can now change how you perceive targets, how you perceive ranges and how you perceive your opponents.

For those of you who think targets are always just targets and backgrounds are just backgrounds, you are right. The diameter of the clay target is constant for all competitors in the event. The distances of the targets are the same for all competitors.

But you have to admit that, targets can play tricks on your eyes from morning light to evening light, seasonal light coloring to seasonal dark coloring and fun competitions to intense ones. Sometimes they appear:

Big (garbage-pail sized) or really small (pill-sized).
Slow or fast.
Invisible in the shadows
or camouflaged by colored leaves.

How does that happen? Is it reality or illusion? Who cares? Let's just fix it.

Skill Drill 15a: Change up your game

You are now going to take advantage of your brain's ability to change things up, just as I did in my karate competition with an iAPP called STRETCH.

Once again, you are going to be the TECH and apply the brilliant way your GO-ZONE allows you to see targets on ideal ranges, and then apply that same kind of brilliance to ranges that frustrate you for any number of reasons—such as sight lines, background, time of day, shadows, malfunctioning trap machines and your attitude that day.

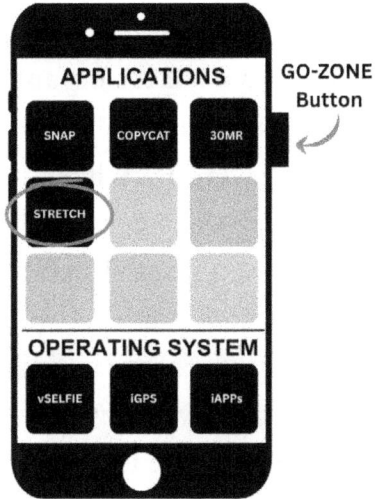

APPLICATIONS

GO-ZONE
Button

SNAP   COPYCAT   3OMR

STRETCH

OPERATING SYSTEM

vSELFIE   iGPS   iAPPs

1. **Imagine a NO-ZONE shooting experience where you saw the target poorly.** Although this image may vary from one reader to the next, there's a good chance you saw the image as small and maybe fast. Perhaps less-bright, a bit fuzzier than usual and maybe even smaller and lacking in color.

2. **Then imagine a GO-ZONE shooting experience where you saw the target brilliantly.** Although the image may vary from one reader to the next, there's a good chance you saw the target as bright, sharp and colorful and maybe even bigger and slower.

3. **Return to the NO-ZONE memory and imagine laying the GO-ZONE image over it (like wallpaper).** Compare the two images. I'm guessing you'll be able to imagine a huge difference.

4. **Now, pretend the NO-ZONE memory is made of playdough and reach out and grab it with both hands.** Stretch, stretch, STRETCH-CH-CH-CH it way out in all directions to the exact same size, brightness, clarity, speed and size of the GO-ZONE memory.

5. **Only one big, garbage pail lid-sized target now remains and it is too big and too slow for you to miss.** Now go to the range and test out your abilities on that type of target.

Be a TECH. While all athletes can visualize this kind of difference, you are one of the few who knows this visual trick of using the STRETCH iAPP to make difficult-to-see targets look like easy-to-see ones.

Use it to change up your image of any target presentation on any range so you can literally love and anticipate presentations that used to evoke fear. You can change shadowy targets at dusk to distinct and clearly obvious midday targets, and change shoot-off targets to be as big as regular round targets.

You can even change other images, such as taking the intense glare of hot summer days and muting it so it appears like the cool sky of a spring day. Test it out and be creative. In your mind, create the targets that you want to see.

Skill Drill 15b: Time-crunch situations

Finally, I've been asked if there is a faster way to do this exercise, as there is a time crunch in most games. Realistically, you have no time to step out of the stand to madly start waving your arms and tinkering with how you see the target. However, there is a faster way, but maybe not in the early stages of your TECH training in this program.

Initially, you'll likely have to use STRETCH after competitions to deal with and clean up your mistakes. (It is part of a debriefing process that we'll discuss in a later chapter.) With this type of TECH debriefing practice, you will get faster and faster at using STRETCH (and other iAPPs) until, amazingly, you'll stop using it altogether—that is, stop using it consciously.

This is because you will have practiced it so much that you'll be using it subconsciously all the time, as the normal skill of the champion you've become. And, by then, it will be so engrained that it'll operate at the speed of light in time-crunch situations.

Next up

In the next chapter, you'll explore the multiple ways you can use your STRETCH iAPP in every kind of sport discipline, and to school and beyond.

Training Tip

Set aside some time to be the TECH and use all of your new iAPPS to improve your game, perhaps by putting one at the top of your daily schedule each day of your week.

Do one hundred mounts while you are in your GO-ZONE.
Use your vSELFIE to win a shoot-off and accept the trophy.
Use SNAP to remove a frustrating memory of a poor event.
Use COPYCAT to learn shoot-off competition skills by stepping into the shoes of your favorite champion. Practice, practice, practice.

"

Courage doesn't mean you don't get afraid.
Courage means you don't let fear stop you.

— BETHANY HAMILTON,
STAR SURFER

"

16
ELIMINATE DISTRACTIONS

Inkball blocks to performance.

"

Obstacles don't have to stop you.
If you run into a wall,
don't turn around and give up.
Figure out how to climb it, go through it,
or work around it.

— MICHAEL JORDAN,
STAR BASKETBALL PLAYER

"

You've come a long way. You've got your GO-ZONE and your operating system with vSELFIE and iGPS for guidance and your iAPPs that enable your ability to be a TECH. You are well on your way to excelling in everything you do, including winning a championship. Congrats. To get full benefit of this program, pull up your calendar on your smart phone and put a different iAPP on every day to remind you to practice them.

The iAPPs in this program are designed to help you get into the GO-ZONE fast by removing NO-ZONE parts of your game. When I was pursuing my black belt in karate, I used them a lot to develop skills and remove blocks in virtually every area of my game, from confidence-building to speed training, from improved agility to lightning-fast reflexes. Foremost, just like every athlete, I required incredible stamina and set in place a running program. But, like most wishful thinking, initially I failed to do it.

"It's dark. It's cold. I'm not a very good runner. My bed's too warm and comfy." And this is where STRETCH provided the solution to overcoming the biggest block to running—me!

Turning adversity into fun

Now the only time I could run was in the morning when the rest of my family was still asleep. It was winter and it was dark. So, I formed an image of the dark morning I was facing. Yuck. I remembered a fun and bright outdoor image of a summer canoe trip. Quite pleasant. Then, with STRETCH, I changed the dark, winter image and made it look like the bright, summer day.

So (almost) smiling, I ventured out into the cold and started to jog, my body immediately hitting the blast of cold air and feeling chilled and tight, as though I'd just walked into a freezer. And I had, as it was -5F (-20C) and who knew what the windchill was. I had dressed in double layers with a one-piece mountaineering suit overtop with a double balaclava or ski mask on my face, so cold should not have been an issue.

With STRETCH, I envisioned the dark, bluey-cold image of the morning. And I envisioned the warm pinkish image of the hot summer's day out playing baseball. Without stopping, I fanned out my arms, as you often see runners doing in a warm up, and used STRETCH to change the dark, bluey-cold image into the pink and warm of summer, and (a bit shocked and pleasantly surprised) I could feel my body relax as I quickened my pace.

All was good, until I came to *the* insurmountable hill. It was a small hill, really, but it looked big at that time in the morning. So I remembered the flat image of the mid-part of the run and how good that had felt.

I overlaid that image on top of the insurmountable-hill image, and used STRETCH to flatten it out and make the hill disappear. Oddly, and effortlessly, my mind seemed to fast-forward in time and I was at the top without effort.

On the home stretch, I was nearing the finish line when a stitch developed in my right side. I imagined the muscles tight and blue. I saw my left-side muscles relaxed and a healthy pink color. Without slowing my speed even slightly, I used STRETCH to change the cramping right-side image to the pinkishness of the left. Amazingly, the pain subsided, euphoria returned and I sprinted the final hundred yards to complete the run.

Skill Drill 16: Conquer your NO-ZONE

Now, I did make that run sound relatively easy, by using STRETCH multiple times to clear away the blocks. And it was, mostly. But running was only a small part of my training. The other major parts of kata forms and free-style fighting required many, many hundreds of iAPP uses to get me over the black-belt grading finish line. Probably even thousands! I encourage you to start using STRETCH and your other iAPPs in every part of your training. What follows are several examples of how you might use

STRETCH for changing, well, everything.

1. **People distractions**

   NO-ZONE: Imagine the image of yourself nervously in a shoot-off or at a world-class event, where perhaps hundreds of people are watching you.

   GO-ZONE: Think of a time when you were telling stories and exchanging jokes with your best friends and having fun.

   Be the TECH: Use STRETCH to change up your on-range presence so you are having as much fun as you do with your friends.

2. **Noise distractions**

   NO-ZONE: Imagine a noisy competition venue with multiple ranges and target chips crashing on the pad beside you, greatly interrupting your focus.

   GO-ZONE: Imagine wading hip deep through a beautiful wilderness stream, casting for trout.

   Be the TECH: Use STRETCH to change your noisy venue into the quietness of a wilderness stream.

3. **Visual distractions**

   NO-ZONE: Imagine a late, late afternoon and the growing dusk at a shoot where the targets are becoming increasingly difficult to see.

   GO-ZONE: Imagine targets that look huge and clear at another time of the day.

   Be the TECH: Use STRETCH to change up your dusky targets and make them crystal clear.

4. **"Hate this range" distractions**

    NO-ZONE: Imagine the image of a range you've shot poorly at and cringe at the thought of competing there.

    GO-ZONE: Imagine a range where you always perform well and love being there.

    Be the TECH: Use STRETCH to change up the NO-ZONE range so it looks like your favorite one.

5. **"Forgot my shotgun" distractions**

    NO-ZONE: Think of a time your shotgun was mistakenly left at home or broke down and you had to borrow one that just looked and felt so wrong.

    GO-ZONE: Imagine your own shotgun, nice and bright with a beautiful halo around it.

    Be the TECH: Use STRETCH to change up your borrowed shotgun so it has the same halo as your own.

6. **"Pain in the shoulder" distractions**

    NO-ZONE: Imagine the image of your shoulder taking a constant beating from repeated shotgun recoil.

    GO-ZONE: Imagine your healthy uninjured shoulder.

    Be the TECH: Use STRETCH to change up your injured shoulder so it looks like your healthy one.

7. **School distractions**

    NO-ZONE: Imagine the image of a school textbook that you have difficulty staying focused on when you read it.

    GO-ZONE: Imagine the image of a book or sport magazine that you love to read (or a video game you love to play).

Be the TECH: Use STRETCH to make the textbook a beautiful masterpiece that you feel you can dive into with the same passion as the book, sport magazine or video game you love.

You'll come across lots of other ways to use your STRETCH iAPP. It's a powerful tool that you should include as a part of your pre-game warmup. Make a regular point of comparing your mental image of the current targets to those of your favorite range.

And then, if you are unhappy with the image, you make the targets huge and slow. I suggest that you physically stretch your arms out as you do the exercise. To others, it'll look like you're warming up arms and shoulders. But for you, you are warming up your mind.

Next up

In the next chapter, you'll add another iAPP that will allow you to change your NO-ZONE physiology (posture) to a GO-ZONE one, in a flash.

Training Tip

Before you go to a new range, head to the internet (with parental permission of course) and find an image of that range. Study the background of the range and compare it to other ranges you've competed or trained at.

Then use your STRETCH iAPP to make that range look bright and appealing, just like your favorite range, so that you "own" it.

And then use your vSELFIE to crush every target in preparation for your competition.

"

Gold medals aren't really made of gold.
They're made of sweat, determination,
and a hard-to-find alloy called guts.

— DAN GABLE,
STAR WRESTLING COACH

"

17
UPLEVEL YOUR POSTURE...

Uplevel your performance.

With practice, you are likely getting a lot better at applying your iAPPS. You are now equipped with an operating system where your GO-ZONE, your vSELFIE and your ability to apply iAPPs by being the TECH starts to work automatically. Even school gets easier!

Everyone will be watching you standing tall and brilliantly smiling in the stand, especially after you use the iAPP that you'll be learning in this chapter.

As a karate competitor, I understood the importance of posture, as I could lose points if my back was even slightly curved or my shoulders rounded. And it took training in front of a bank of mirrors at the YMCA to help me further identify the importance of this and ensure that my form never failed me.

In one memorable training session, I was rather enjoying using the dance-studio mirrors, as it was the first time I'd ever seen myself perform with such immediate feedback. When I got to a key powerful "show-off" move in my kata form, I unleashed my signature, intense karate yell directly in front of my image—and froze.

My form was a disaster. My hips were bowed to the right of my body in total misalignment to my shoulders—by about four inches! It just looked weird. How, I asked myself, had this gone unnoticed for this long? The mirrors were clearly good honest iGPS feedback.

As you now know, your COPYCAT iAPP is used for copying excellence. And you also know that they can accidentally copy bad posture, technique or form. Well, I began to wonder whose bad posture I had copied—my father, my mother, my grandmother? Who knew? Simply, I'd developed a sideways S-curve, called a lordosis. No wonder I lost points in competition. No wonder I had back pain.

As I watched myself in the mirror, I consciously inched my hips over so that they aligned with my shoulders. And did that ever feel a weird kind of good. But it made no long-term difference, as on the next run-through of my form, my hips sprang back out of alignment. Long story short, with a lot of work using these iAPPs, I was able to fix this curvature of my spine and it clearly paid off competitively in medal-winning form.

Change your posture

It is a challenge for anyone to stay in the GO-ZONE with poor posture. Slouching tightens up your back muscles and prevents your technique from being consistent, as it hinders your fluid movement to the target.

It impacts your breathing. It impacts your strength and power. With a slouched posture, whom you copied no longer matters. You can and have to fix it.

Skill Drill 17: Replace ineffective physiology

You may be familiar with how snowboarders talk about "shredding" the mountain, a term that implies the application of power and finesse on those fast, mountain traversing sweeps across and down the face of the slope. We're going to use this same term to describe how you'll build a powerful posture and physiology by shredding the slumped-over hangdog NO-ZONE postures.

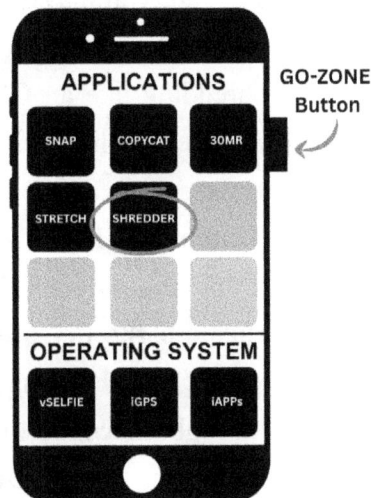

1. **Imagine a NO-ZONE problem you have in a specific area of your game,** at the beginning, after a poor round or, very specifically, in a particular stand.
2. **Imagine that NO-ZONE image of yourself in the middle of a huge TV screen.**

That *"you"* is likely in a diminished posture, perhaps with rounded shoulders with the look of defeat. Needless to say, unless something changes, that *'you'* is potentially going to miss several more targets. A postural adjustment may be in order.

3. **And it's SHREDDER to the rescue!** SHREDDER is actually YOU, the GO-ZONE version of you at a time when you crushed clays easily. This *you*, as SHREDDER, appears on one side of the TV screen with the powerful, dynamic posture of a GO-ZONE winner.

    For fun, you may even imagine a superhero cape flying out behind SHREDDER, strapped to a snowboard, and shredding like an Olympian. Totally upright in posture, muscles rippling, wicked smile on the face—the form and finesse are scary good.

4. **Watch *you* in SHREDDER mode sweep powerfully from one side of the TV screen to the other, right through the defeated *you* in the center, to the other side.** Then, turning, watch SHREDDER travel back through the centre image again. With each sweep across the screen, SHREDDER powers through *you* in the middle and you start to notice that your form and posture adjusts and takes on the image and power of SHREDDER.

    Continue this process until the (formerly defeated) *you* in the middle is the spitting image of the posture and form of SHREDDER.

5. **Then, combine both images into one. Marvel at the new posture and imagine stepping into the shoes of this revitalized *you*.** Taller. Stronger. Faster reflexes. Upright posture. With a determined smile on your face. The GO-ZONE returns and you are ready to shred the targets on any range.

You can use SHREDDER in any NO-ZONE situation—in clays and in life. It is my go-to when a client phones me in a state of panic in the middle of an event, as it always gets them back into the GO-ZONE quickly.

One such client was on the verge of losing her Olympic dream and SHREDDER basically shredded the lethargy that threatened her Olympic opportunity, and helped her to dominate the selection event in the match final. Like her, I encourage you to fire up SHREDDER in NO-ZONE moments of desperation and let it do its work.

SHREDDER can also be used in real time and applied to your fitness program, to change your posture such as I did and to deal with the result of bad posture—pain. In addition to my use of the STRETCH iAPP on my training runs, I often placed my NO-ZONE blocks ahead of me on the road and shredded right through it.

In some clays sports you can do the same by walking through mistakes and shredding them as you move from stand to stand. In seconds, SHREDDER refreshes and rejuvenates you, as though the mistake or letdown never happened.

Next up

In the next chapter, we'll use SHREDDER to help in a totally different way, one that is designed to keep you in your GO-ZONE for a long day of competing, no matter how many delays or problems you might face.

Training Tip

Fatigue is a great interrupter of the GO-ZONE, because it often has a long history of showing up in sport, school and other activities. That means it is well practiced.

But the next time you start to yawn just before or during the round, place yourself out on the SHREDDER screen and quickly run your SHREDDER iAPP. The *you* in the center of the stage will be happy you did, and the wide-awake "surgery" of your posture will be effective.

18
PREPARE FOR COMPETITION

Ramp up performance readiness.

> "
> *Some people say I have attitude. Maybe I do...*
> *but I think you have to. You have to believe in*
> *yourself when no one else does.*
> *That makes you a winner right there.*
>
> **— VENUS WILLIAMS,**
> STAR TENNIS PLAYER

"

In the heat of summer or the coolness of spring or fall, you have to stay focused and in your GO-ZONE. Any of your new iAPPS can be used to keep you on track. Keep making yourself as big as a mountain with your vSELFIE and fixing your weaknesses with your iAPPs as the best TECH on the range. Now you've also got SHREDDER to rescue you in any situation. But there is one more trick up SHREDDER's sleeve.

One of my high-performance athletes in hockey finished his final development year of amateur play and nobody called. Except one coach who allowed him to try out as a favor to the player's father, the expectation being that he'd get his opportunity and go away with a bit of self-esteem that he had at least tried.

As an exceptional player with exceptional tenacity, he made the cut. But that was almost the end of his hockey story, as when the season started, he was mostly sitting on and "warming" the bench. When we met up in our usual meeting, I asked him how he felt about that.

"Frustrated," he answered. "I could really help the team."

I said, "So you are sitting on the bench frustrated and probably bored, and the coach finally puts you in the game. How are you going to play?"

His head went down. "You got me," he said. "Not good."

I told him that his job on the bench was to be in his GO-ZONE all the time, engaged in the play mentally and physiologically, ready and always looking to the coach to be put in on the next shift. If he did that, I told him, he'd demonstrate what he could really do, full throttle, full GO-ZONE, full leadership.

So I taught him another use for the SHREDDER, that of ensuring that his physiology was absolutely ready to perform at any moment. And, within just one week, he earned a full-time shift on a high-level hockey team, headed in the right direction for a pro career.

Skill Drill 18: Be a powerful moving target

Think of a time when you had a delay in your game because of rain or lightning or because of a slow squad ahead of you. Long gone is the adrenaline you built up in your 30MR. Long gone is your GO-ZONE as you started chatting with your squad mates. Long gone is your reason for being there—to win!

You are fighting against being too social with others who have no idea how being social undermines their game. The heat of the day may be making you sleepy. Your stomach may be growling. Time to be the TECH and call on SHREDDER, that high-performance *you* with unlimited adrenaline.

This time, we are going to shorten up the shredding, as instead of a long sweep of SHREDDER across the image, this time we are simply going to sway or shuffle back and forth through the image of SHREDDER.

To make this more realistic, stand up as you do this exercise and pretend you are on the range.

1. **Imagine yourself in a situation where your competition is delayed and you've lost your GO-ZONE.** Whether it's the heat, long days of competition or too many NO-ZONE athletes around you, your energy levels have plummeted to zero.

2. **Right beside you in this dilemma, imagine SHREDDER, the high-performance image of you.** SHREDDER is nearly on top of you, only a couple of inches from your body centerline, but it is no less powerful.

   Remember that SHREDDER is *you* at your best—strong, powerful, effective—so personal closeness is important! It's you at a brilliant moment in your game. Your performance was easy. Every target was inkballed. This is *you*; this is SHREDDER.

3. **Now shift (or shuffle) from foot to foot, like a swaying tree, back and forth.**
   As you do, drift through the image of SHREDDER, back and forth. Keep swaying back and forth through this imagined SHREDDER image. With each passage, you should notice an intensifying GO-ZONE. With lots of adrenaline!
   Let this feeling further intensify with each sway, along with a quieting mind and zero self-talk. Embrace this quietness. The increase in energy is usually amazing.

4. **Sustain SHREDDER.** Right up to the moment you step back into the stand, do your pre-shot routine and then crush'em.

5. **Return to your swaying after you're finished in the stand.** And never, never stop, until you are ready to step into the next stand.

When you are shifting through SHREDDER, you stop thinking and your mind becomes quiet. Plus, it engages your mirror neurons and prevents them from locking into anyone else's frustration, nervousness or bad form.

Most professional athletes shift in this manner. You'll especially notice it at the start of games during the anthem. It allows them to keep their bodies engaged and ready, in the same way my hockey player learned to apply it when he was tired of "warming the bench."

As well, use SHREDDER at the start of your competitive day, especially before your rounds as part of your 30MR. Be sure to let your coach and parents know why you are using this iAPP, so they can understand the importance of you moving and that it is not just "nerves."

They can also let you know with a prearranged signal that you have stopped moving and might want to resume. Your consistent GO-ZONE depends on it.

Next up

In the next chapter, we'll look at how getting and staying fit helps you to stay consistent both in technique and adrenaline.

Training Tip

When you are doing SHREDDER, keep your eyes on the horizon (or the pretend horizon if your view is obscured by trees or buildings).

This should completely eliminate the self-talk that is so common during the 30MR preparation period. Your brain will be quiet, your eyes will be quiet and your body will be ready. Crazy ready!

"
*In shooting events, a lot of endurance
is required. If your body is fit, then you will
be mentally fit as well. I started working out,
put on some muscle, and my performance started
getting better. I felt fresh and, of course, saw some
positive changes in my body, which also helped
with endurance for competing under the hot sun
all day. [As edited by Bob Palmer]*

—A.S. NARUKA
STAR SKEET SHOOTER
"

19
MAKE FITNESS FUN

Build long-lasting endurance for competition.

> " *If you want to be the best, you have to do things other people aren't willing to do.* "
>
> **— MICHAEL PHELPS**
> STAR SWIMMER

In the last few chapters you learned and applied SHREDDER. You now know the importance of posture and how to sustain it by shifting from side-to-side through SHREDDER. You are becoming the TECH expert on how to maintain all things GO-ZONE. Your program of excellence is certainly starting to come together. Trust the process.

Sometimes a lack of energy (lethargy or sleepiness) makes your GO-ZONE difficult to sustain, and that is often your body speaking, not your mind. One of the best ways to ensure you stay fully alert and wired to win at clays is to develop your fitness level, which, of course, plays out in your stamina and your ability to sustain high levels of adrenaline.

Simply, your body is crying out and saying, "Help me get strong and fit for those long, hot summer days." And that makes it so much easier to stay consistently in your GO-ZONE.

Olympic shooting sports used to be played by all manner of athletes in all manner of shapes, sizes and fitness levels. But around 2000, a whole new group of young athletes started to take over the sport. They were amazing in their shooting skill, their GO-ZONE that drove them and, especially, their high fitness level. Within a few years they changed the clays game to a game of perfect. And now, at the highest levels of clays shooting, the excellent physical fitness of clays shooters is indistinguishable from that of other Olympic athletes.

Benefits of fitness

Just so you know, other than just being buff, fitness gives you many more benefits than you may think. While I mentioned stamina, the list also includes healthy lung capacity (with excellent oxygen metabolization), strength, agility, flexibility, injury prevention, better injury recovery, better focus, better vision, clearer thinking, healthy body image, self-esteem, better sleep and digestion, general wellness via an improved immune response, better body temperature regulation and the list goes on and on.

Fitness also gives a huge boost in mental well-being. It will buoy you up as one of your lifelong pleasures and be a great social connector. And, I'm told, it will help you to live longer. But enough of that, as, primarily, it will give you the stamina to win and win big.

Those long hot, skin-drying, eye-tearing, windy summer days, with day after day of searing concentration will be joyful and even euphoric. Struggles with fatigue will be a thing of the past. Your mind supports you. Your body supports you. The writing is on the wall. The fitter men and women are dominating the podium. Are you in or out?

Skill Drill 19: Get fit and build stamina

I encourage all of my athletes to get fit. The son of a former national-level college champion, developed a weekly strength workout program based on his father's past training. And that year, along with all the other training and shooting skills he was learning, he outlasted the best in the U.S. and won the trap event at the national high-school championship.

As I write this, he is in great form (and shape) and preparing for his last big events of his senior year, as well as applying to colleges that have a clays program. As a clays shooter, you may not have a former national college wrestling champion to help you to set up a training program, and you'll likely have to set up your own program, but you may need to get others, such as your parents, involved. And they may join in and train with you.

Here are four things you can do to get started:

1. **Get involved in a school or recreational sport.** There's lots of opportunity to get fit where games are fun and getting fit can be effortless. It can also be a training ground to improve your GO-ZONE.

2. **Talk to your coach about getting your whole team doing fitness together.** Or, maybe you'll have to be the leader and start a workout group on your own.

3. **Plan your fitness training with your coach, parents and physician (if applicable) and build up gradually.** Over the program, increase your number of workouts and the intensity of them. And then taper them as you get closer to competitions.

4. **Buy a good pair of running shoes for the gym or track,** as you already know from your clays training, good equipment matters.

As an extra boost, use your vSELFIE to see yourself buff and fit and able to last a long and intense day of competing. Use your COPYCAT iAPP to copy Olympians and pros and research what they do to stay fit. Use STRETCH and SHREDDER to break through blocks. Be patient with your progress, as getting fit and building the kind of stamina you need may take a little time. But as you now know, the benefits are worth it.

Now, on those long hot days when others are whining, complaining and looking for excuses for dropped targets, you will be feeling your GO-ZONE with ample stamina. Believe me, your body will be thanking you, with the gift of a never-ending GO-ZONE.

Next up

Before you dive into the next chapter, spend some practice time using your GO-ZONE and your operating system of vSELFIE, iGPS and iAPPs. Be the TECH. And, while fitness helps you to support your GO-ZONE with endurance and many other benefits, you are going to learn to manage your GO-ZONE for a whole day, from the start to finish, so that you are always ready and letting nothing throw you off of that readiness.

Training Tip

Developing your fitness can be fun as you'll feel so much better. But getting started can be a chore if none of your teammates or friends ever train for fitness.

So, I want you to stop thinking of fitness as fitness. Instead, I want you to think of it as leadership. When you become a winner you stand out. People watch and admire you. They want to be just like you and be winners too.

But to be a winner, you have to be a leader and at the top of the podium, which is also called the *leader*board. But why wait? Be the first to start a fitness program. Be the leader and stand out now.

" "

The miracle isn't that I finished.
The miracle is that I had the courage to start.

—JOHN BINGHAM,
STAR RUNNER

20
MANAGE YOUR COMPETITIVE DAY

Create a game plan for winning.

There are only two options regarding commitment. You're either IN or you're OUT. There is no such thing as life in-between.

— PAT RILEY,
STAR SPORT-TEAM PRESIDENT

Up to now, I've lightened up your competitive pressure with a program for excelling and winning. Except for me having you stand on your head, I've had you doing just about everything else from powerful walking to powerful shifting to pinching and copycatting and stretching targets.

So in this chapter, I thought I'd press the pause button and do something a little different, and walk you through a competition.

By now, with your diligent practicing of the tools and iAPPs of this program, I'm expecting that you are enjoying clays competitions more and even showing your friends, family and coach what you are capable of.

Your GO-ZONE should see you maintaining consistency, gaining more targets and upping your averages. Your vSELFIE should be building excitement and limiting nervousness. Your iGPS should be guiding you pretty routinely now with limited blowups and limited anger and a more gentle approach to putting shell hulls in the bins.

And you have a very good group of iAPPS that you can use in your role as TECH. Put on coveralls, get your hands busy and use your tools to correct weak parts of your game.

Nobody has a silver bullet for instant success. The reality is that you'll likely fail a lot, fix a lot of mistakes with iAPPS and practice your vSELFIEs many hundreds of times before you become a champion. As TECH, you'll get a lot of practice in your sport, school and life.

Skill Drill 20: Manage your competition day

The tools you use and how you use them may vary depending on the time of day you start your competition, as well as how long your competition goes for. So, we'll look at managing your day before, during and after your competition, and address when to use your new iAPPs.

1. Be prepared for competition

First, you'll need a checklist for getting your equipment ready, ensuring everything is present and accounted for. You'll need lots of water for hot days, as well as sunscreen. Now, mom or dad may be preparing all this stuff for you, plus getting you out of bed, packed and on the road, but don't blame them for leaving something behind. It is time for you to start taking over this responsibility—as it is all part of your training. A simple checklist is all you need.

Second, competition day is too late for asking your coach for technical changes and competition day is way too late to do panicky visualizations. Very little can be learned in the week before a competition, let alone the morning of the competition.

So give your panic a rest and enjoy the process. Really enjoy it, as you've done the best you can do. You have to trust that you are ready. Because at the end of this competition, you'll likely have lots of exciting changes (iGPS) to work on before the next one.

2. Get a good start to your day

Waking up is so much easier when you've gotten to bed early and feel rested. You jump out of bed and immediately check in with your GO-ZONE. It feels good. Or it doesn't. So you become the TECH and use your SNAP iAPP and get your GO-ZONE back.

You dive into the shower and afterwards check in with your GO-ZONE. It feels good. Or it doesn't. So you become the TECH and step into the shoes of a champion and use your COPYCAT iAPP.

You wolf down your breakfast (a healthy one) and you check in with your GO-ZONE again. It still feels good. You are getting the idea. It should always feel good, but never be ramped up like a crazy, runaway horse.

3. On the road and at the range

On the drive to the range your GO-ZONE still feels good, or it doesn't and you again become the TECH and fix it using SHREDDER, by crushing through the NO-ZONE on that TV screen, a dozen times or more.

At the range, you chat with friends you haven't seen for a year and a little bell goes off in your head (or your parents remind you) that your round starts in an hour. You put your equipment together and a crazy good GO-ZONE feeling begins to course through your veins.

All those vSELFIE sessions you have done have worked really well to get you ready, and you are pumped up with adrenaline. You feel nicely wired. Some call this feeling NERVES, you know that it is you building your GO-ZONE and getting ready. That wiredness feels normal.

4. Get your mind ready

You know what to do as the time ticks closer to the start of your competition and that means starting your 30MR.

1. **Put on the imaginary horse blinders** and talk to no one, not even your coach or parents.
2. **Stay in your intense Zone, swaying back and forth** through SHREDDER with your eyes on the horizon.
3. **Intensely vSELFIE your first round** so it feels like you are actually pulling the trigger, with imaginary adrenaline blasting out of your imaginary barrels.

4. **Be sure to use your STRETCH iAPP** to stretch out the imaginary targets so they look like garbage pail lids and are unmissable.

When you do all this in your 30MR time period, crushing your first round will feel like déjà vu. You'll feel intensely comfortable. Really comfortable. Like wired comfortable.

5. Manage your downtime between events

Let's not rush eating lunch. Of course, mom, dad or you packed a nutritious lunch. If you plan to donate to the club or the food truck by eating burgers and fries, be prepared to struggle harder to keep your GO-ZONE. Just saying, because fast food is heavy food that may make you feel heavy, sleepy and slow. You want to support your GO-ZONE, not undermine it.

And, if you have a lot of time after lunch or between events (one or two hours), grab a rest in the car. Set your alarm so that you know when to start your 30MR and ramp back up for the next round or event.

6. Wind down and prepare for the next day

As you have planned and executed your day well, you'll be tired but excited for the success you'll be having tomorrow. It's a good time to review the day and be a TECH. Perhaps you'll use a couple of iAPPS to fix a blip that occurred in your performance before taking the off-ramp for the night.

You enjoy dinner with your friends or family. You do a vSELFIE right after supper so you'll be ready for the next day's performance. And you go to bed on time. For sure, you'll be rested and ready for the next day. Bring it on! But as usually happens, you're asleep before your head hits the pillow—z-z-z-z-z-z-z-z.

Next up

In the next chapter, we'll get back to work, and you'll learn how to pump yourself up with a powerful but level-headed amount of adrenaline. Forget having a beverage of some sugary liquid spiked with caffeine, as it's money poorly spent. Your own adrenaline is way better—no additives needed. Next you'll learn a new iAPP to manage your level of wiredness, all day long.

There are a lot of influences at competitions that drain your energy, very similar to how leaving your truck lights on drains the battery.

Training Tip

Eating heavy food, being around nervous or sleepy squadmates, enduring oppressively hot weather conditions, missing a good night's sleep, trying to stay focused after taking allergy medication, or playing endless video games on a cell phone.

There is no good solution to these except to never complain and never accept any of these as excuses. Fight back, as every time you overcome one of these types of drains on your GO-ZONE, you get stronger (and smarter). After a while, when you avoid or dominate these energy-draining experiences, you'll be the one standing on the podium!

"

When you're in the moment [the Zone],
your mind and body work together
to create a perfect shot.

— KIM RHODE,
STAR SKEET SHOOTER

"

21
WIRE YOURSELF FOR SUCCESS

Harness the power of adrenaline.

> " *Relax? How can anybody relax and play golf?*
> *You have to grip the club, don't you?* "
>
> — **BEN HOGAN,**
> STAR GOLFER

Your toolkit is expanding way beyond trying to relax, breathe or pretend to be happy. You are a budding athletic TECH who will keep working toward success no matter what the block to performance. Whenever you run into a block or a problem, you now have a choice of iAPPS from which to choose.

In the previous chapter you experienced how all of these iAPPs might be applied to your next competition. Now, you'll add the missing ingredient. Pizzazz! Or most people would call it adrenaline.

Imagine calling pull and pulling your trigger. You hear a muffled pop and the pellets sputter out of the barrel and scatter a dozen feet from you on the ground. Meanwhile, the target is long gone. Oops, someone put too little powder in that shell—loss!

Now you may find this impossible to imagine, because powder is usually an exact amount in every shell in an exacting manufacturing process. But what if you could never be sure?

What if the powder varied from shot to shot? Round to round? Competition to competition? You know as well as I do that you could never trust your hold point, your breakpoint or anything else, for that matter. Your game would never even get started.

In the same way, your level of adrenaline needs to be as absolutely certain to you as the level of powder in your shell. You need adrenalized consistency, because it gives you the exact amount of wiredness that will carry you through a full day of competing, regardless of the weather, the level of competition or the time of day. Adrenaline is what stabilizes your game. So your level of adrenaline needs to be very high—higher than you can probably imagine.

Find the right amount of adrenaline

The amount of adrenaline you require varies from activity to activity. Reading a book (and staying engaged without yawning and having to reread paragraphs) is quite different from the amount you need for total focus under competitive conditions in your game.

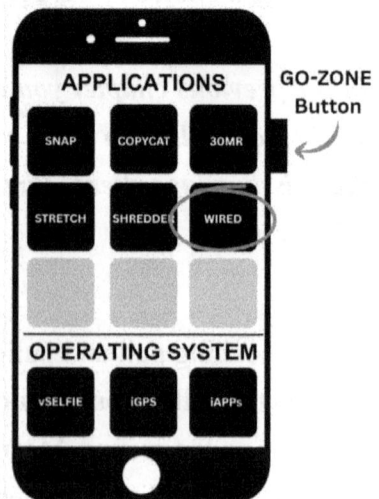

Now you can perform very well in your GO-ZONE when you are calm (book reading level). And that is what many athletes are repeatedly told—to be calm! But calm only works in calm practice. Calm only works on calm days. Calm only works when nobody is watching or bugging you.

As a matter of fact, in the wind, during rain storms, calm rarely works. On difficult ranges with lousy trap machines and poor sight lines, calm rarely works. In finals, at national championships, when qualifying for Olympic placements, calm rarely works.

With the after-effects of a sleepless night, upset stomach, the runs or stuffy-nose, cold symptoms, calm rarely works. Even reading this chapter requires a consistent level of adrenaline. Adrenaline is your super-charged powder and you need to learn to make it explode consistently.

Skill Drill 21: Deliver consistent adrenaline

To help you to build a consistent level of adrenaline, you are going to create a button for adrenaline with a new iAPP called WIRED. It will fuel your GO-ZONE.

1. **Write out a list of adrenalized and exciting experiences you've had such as:**
   - Being on a rollercoaster where you were enjoyably scared
   - Winning a clays or other sport competition
   - Visiting your favorite crazy friends
   - Watching your favorite sports team win

- Viewing your favorite (edge-of-your-seat) TV series or movie
- Getting the autograph of your favorite athlete

2. **Select a spot on your hand for your WIRED iAPP button.** I'm going to suggest the webbing between your thumb and index finger. If you are right-handed, pick the webbing on your left hand. If you are left-handed, pick the webbing on your right. This spot is going to trigger your WIRED iAPP and loads of adrenaline.

3. **Now, think of the first experiences you listed, and feel (really feel!) the excitement that it generates.** With your other hand, pinch the webbing between your thumb and index finger. Hold it for 15 seconds while continuing to think of the totally-wired experience.

   Think of the second experience, and feel the excitement it generates (I mean really jump-up-and-down feel it!) and pinch the webbing on your hand. Hold for 15 seconds. Complete all of your listed experiences in this manner. You are layering many great adrenalized experiences into this button.

4. **Now, shadow box around your rec room, bedroom or on a trampoline (safely) and imagine fighting opponents intensely, in the manner I suggested in Chapter 5, *Dial in for Success,* with your vSELFIE.** Increase your level of excitement to crazy, fun levels,

but be careful of breakable objects around the room. If a calm GO-ZONE is book-reading level 1, and a highly-adrenalized GO-ZONE is a whopping shoot-off level 10, you want to go for level 10 or more! When you feel your level 10, firmly press your WIRED button on your hand.

5. **Rest for five minutes and repeat step 4.** Rest again for five minutes and repeat step 4.

6. **The test. Now think of a boring experience, one where you can immediately feel your energy diminish.** You'll feel the NO-ZONE creep back in when you think of it. But hey, if you want to be a top clays athlete and you are losing concentration in competition, you are in trouble. To get your GO-ZONE level 10 back, press your WIRED button and notice the shift. It should feel good. Very good. And wired!

Your WIRED button should have triggered your Zone. If so, way to go! You now have a new and important tool. If pressing it produces a weak response or none at all, go back through the exercise and redo it, as adrenaline is so-o-o-o-o-o-o important. You can also incorporate intense running, wind sprints, skipping and karate screams. Firmly press WIRED and be a bit crazy.

And for those of you who feel that you are way too wired, only you can know how much you really need. That said, wait until you get a windy, rainy day where the trap machines fail every five targets, or you feel a little under the weather with a queasy stomach, because then you'll need every shot of adrenaline you can eke out of your body. Ironically, the WIRED iAPP will actually help you to understand how high levels of adrenaline can actually feel calm.

From here on in, during every round, you need to be an adrenalized level-10 GO-ZONE. From your 30MR, through the first round, all the way to the last round and match finals, you must be fueled with adrenaline. No exceptions. Just like your shells need to have consistent powder, so does your body need to have consistent adrenaline. And from here on in, it is up to you to build your WIRED iAPP and use it.

Next up

In the next chapter, I'll help you to better understand your WIRED iAPP, and how it will assist you to excel in competition and in everything you do. Because adrenaline matters and its consistency is what turns a good competitor into a champion.

Training Tip

Now that you have your WIRED iAPP installed, it may need to be charged up from time to time as using it over time may wear it down and drain it of its power.

So, every time you have an exciting experience or success in your sport (or life), press your WIRED button to add that extra feeling of energy. Layer it on, over and over, and pretty soon it will work automatically for you. Hands-free.

22
BE AN ENGINEER

Design your adrenaline flow.

> "
>
> *Design is not how it looks like and feels like.*
> *Design is how it works.*
>
> **— STEVE JOBS,**
> STAR COMPUTER GUY
>
> "

Am I ever excited by how far you have come. Whether you get on the podium or not in your upcoming competitions, you need to take notice of what works and what doesn't, and use all of the incredible iGPS feedback to improve your game. I'm proud of you.

In the previous chapter, you added the WIRED iAPP to access one-stop adrenaline. In this chapter, you'll get to manage your energy levels even better.

You probably love roller coaster rides. They slowly take you to the top of the hill and then let you travel at breakneck speeds where your stomach feels crazy good and crazy excited. Up and down and around. And then it is over. But you get on it again and slowly rise to the top and experience the up and down gravitational pull all over again. [Imagine the excited screams.]

Now a roller coaster is fun and a little scary, and the up and down unplanned nature of it is part of the fun. That being out of control is what makes it scary and an even greater part of the fun. Except, what is good for scary roller coasters is not so good for you on the range or during a competition.

Being up and down and out of control in a competition can mean disaster. You may get too excited and take your head off the stock and jump at the target. You may get too relaxed and the blur of the target never seems to focus and you are stabbing at the target and playing target catch-up.

Engineer your adrenaline

To be ready, you'll need to manage the adrenaline you built with your WIRED iAPP, so that it is constant, rather than an up and down unplanned roller coaster ride. Unlike riding a roller coaster, you need to be in control. And unlike the roller coaster, you need to manage your game from wake-up to bedtime in order to stay in your GO-ZONE under all conditions.

So far in this program, I've asked you to be an archaeologist, an engineer, a navigator, a technician, a scientist and an architect. Now I'd like you to be an engineer again, so that you can design how your day unfolds. Because if you design it well, you'll know where the hills and valleys and curves are, so that you can manage your adrenaline when you need it.

You have to be fired up and ready when you wake up on competition day, when you step into the stand and when you call pull. But then you have to ease off of your adrenaline just a bit between shots, during breaks in the action and, especially, when it is time to wind down and go to sleep to be fully rested for the next day.

Skill Drill 22: Design your perfect day to control your game

We still want a roller coaster in our game, but we want to design it—like an engineer might design a real roller coaster. You'll be designing your perfect day starting with getting out of bed, right through to turning out your light at night.

1. **You wake up in the morning on competition days, and you start your designed roller coaster ride.** During breakfast, it's a nice gentle climb, not too steep, but trending upward (and certainly not trending downward).

2. **On the way to the range, the climb gets higher and the adrenaline gets more intense.** But, at any time if the adrenaline runs away on you, you simply throttle it back. You need to stay in charge.

3. **Now at the range, the 30MR kicks in and you shift to the top of your adrenaline and to the top of the ride,** teetering on the edge, a smile on your face, visualizing the first round with your vSELFIE at full throttle, ready to go.

4. **You step onto the first stand and the momentum takes you through the shot.** Smoked'em.

5. **You have a few seconds to ease off on the adrenaline just a little,** before cranking it back up for the next shot. Smoked'em.

You've now engineered an intense, wavy, up and down (sine curve) process to take you through all the shots on that stand or round. You finish your last shot, sign the score card and engineer the roller coaster to drop back down in a managed decline, as you step off the range. In this relaxed mode, you rest and recover. Then you prepare for your next round or stand, or pack up and finish for the day.

And that is you being the engineer, where you design and implement your engineered, adrenalized ride. You have the perfect intensity where and when you need it. It is a very efficient process. If at any time your engineered ride falters, you simply use your WIRED button to give yourself a boost.

And if at any time your engineered roller coaster is acting like a runaway train—perhaps at night when you are trying to fall asleep—you can use iAPPS like SNAP or SHREDDER in reverse to slow it down, by using relaxing memories in your life, like times at the beach or at the fishing hole.

Now, by using your vSELFIE, design your perfect roller coaster ride, from getting up in the morning on competition day to going to sleep. Sorry, I forgot a step. From getting up, to performing and excelling, to sleeping. Be an engineer with your adrenaline. You can give up control and be frenzied or lethargic, or you can design your perfect day.

Next up

In the next chapter we'll look at how to make all those scary, noisy, intimidating and bothersome people disappear. You've been an archaeologist, technician, architect and an engineer, and now you'll be a wizard!

Training Tip

After having designed your perfect day and your perfect performance where the rollercoaster is managed and controlled, you'll be able to identify where it goes off the rails— so you can change up your day where you need to.

This could be anything from who you drive to the competition with, what you eat during the competition and whom you hang out with. Expensive energy drinks are often the substance of choice for athletes to get themselves wired, but when you learn to do it on your own via your adrenaline and your WIRED iAPP, you'll be way more consistent and save some money in the process.

"

You don't just want to beat a team. You want to leave a lasting impression in their minds.

— MIA HAMM,
Star Soccer Player

"

23
BE A WIZARD

"Disappear" opponents.

> *It's not how big you are, but how big you play.*
>
> **— JOHN WOODEN,**
> STAR COACH

You are well on your way to being a champion, by managing your GO-ZONE and ensuring you stay in it via all of your new iAPP strategies that you can apply with the genius of a TECH.

After reading about, installing and using the WIRED iAPP, you should be very adrenalized with a highly-engineered competition day. I'd expect your game-day consistency to be way, way up.

But there is an important thing you still have to do. You have to deal with all of those pesky opponents who expect you to falter so they can beat you. In order to do that, you are going to become a wizard, along with the other roles that I've asked you to pretend to be. By the time you are finished reading this chapter, you'll be able to wave your wand and make your opponents disappear—and maybe your bothersome brother or sister, too!

Opponents are distractions

In the Training Tip at the end of Chapter 13, Bob's 30-Minute Rule, I asked you to partner up with a friend, face to face and to try to keep a straight, unsmiling face. I'm guessing that you found that hard to do. You and your mirror neurons (of which you had no idea of their existence at the time) had no defense. After only a few seconds, you were likely both laughing.

In clays competitions, if someone is trying to get you to smile by teasing or non-stop talking, or, perhaps, irritating you to the point of frustration and anger, you are experiencing the importance of having a 30MR for protection. It ensures you have a buffer zone, and, in doing so, you protect yourself (and your mirror neurons) from human distraction.

But once you are on the range and the rounds have started, getting away from others for 30 minutes is impossible, as they'll be standing right beside you, and behind you, and on all of the other ranges around you.

Their voices may throw you off, as some competitors call for the target in weird ways. Their actions may throw you off, as some smack their shells into the bin. Some mutter. Some slouch. Others display terrible, even horrible form. So it is more important than ever to block out all of this distracting stuff, even when your competitors are staring you in the face.

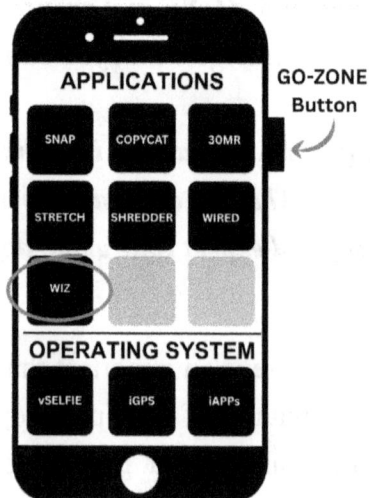

In any competition, just the thought of competing against others can mess with your mind. On the official practice day of an international world cup, where no scoring is done, many competitors perform below their potential.

The perceived pressure is on, and, for whatever reason, even though they still have the same, perfect score as everyone else, they are bothered by their competitors. And nobody has even dropped or lost a target yet. The scoreboard is blank. It is only a practice round, people!

But when you come to think of it, that is the point of competitions. You pit yourself against everyone else from across the country to see who is the best in one event on one site. Otherwise, everyone could just compete at their home ranges, compile the scores nationwide and save a lot of money on travel expenses.

So, the most skillful technical competitor can lose. While skill still counts, the skillful competitor who can best block out their rivals is the one who wins. In competition, the better you get at "not seeing your opponents," the better you'll perform.

To block out your opponents so that you only see the target, you will need to become a wizard, much like Harry Potter or his friend Hermione, where you make your opponents disappear. You tap your wand, say your spell and poof, a cloud of white smoke forms. When it disappears, you are all alone in the stand.

> **No competitors, coaches, parents or spectators.**
> **No pressure.**
> **Just great big targets sitting up**
> **in the sky waiting to be crushed.**

Skill Drill 23: "Disappear" your opponents for total focus

With your WIZ iAPP (which you may have guessed is short for wizard) you get to create a kind of magic by creatively using your mind to remove people distractions.

1. **Pick a Bothersome Person (BP) who can negatively affect your game.** (The BP might be angry, loud, bullying, etc.)

2. **Imagine that you are watching a huge TV screen.** Put the BP character on one side of the screen. See the BP with the bothersome behavior, such as being irritating, angry, loud or bullying.

3. **Next, put yourself, as the second character, on the other side of the TV screen,** where you may look distracted and display emotions such as anger, frustration or unhappiness as a result of the BP's disruptive behavior.

4. **Watch the drama of the two characters.** Then, as Harry or Hermione might do, pretend to tap an imaginary wand a couple of times and point it at *you* on the screen and start turning *you* into a giant, 10 feet tall or even taller. As you imagine yourself growing in size, notice that the BP may

possibly be shrinking like the water-soaked Wicked Witch of *the West in The Wizard of Oz.* ("Help! I'm melting.")

5. **When that *you* on the screen is as big as a giant, and the BP is the size of an ant, put your wand away and imagine standing in your shoes on the screen.** Look around to see if the BP is anywhere. They might just have completely disappeared. Puff! Gone.

Congratulations on using WIZ and being the wizard. It is way too easy and so powerful. Harry and Hermione would be proud of you. Now you just have to test it out at a practice or competition.

I have a rule, one of Bob's rules that says:

If you can see your opponents (when they are irritating or intimidating), they have beaten you.

In other words, you have let your opponent get into your head. So, for homework, use WIZ to "disappear" all of your opponents, as well as your squadmates, parents, coaches, officials. You want no distractions of any human kind when you are performing. That way, you'll only see targets!

Do this and you'll perform a whole lot more consistently, just as though you are the only person on the range. It is not about controlling them. You are simply not letting them control you. And one more thing, when an athlete gets back from a competition I'll ask them a trick question:

"How did your squadmates perform?"

And I think you now know the response that I expect.

"What squadmates?"

Next up

With WIZ, you'll become a leader and move to the top of the standings list. Because you know what the list is called in most sports. The leaderboard. And to get to the top of the *leader*board, you are going to need to learn to be a leader in both sport and life. In the next chapter, you'll stay with being a wizard and learn to deal with bothersome people in your life so that you are never intimidated.

Training Tip

Your WIZ iAPP is one of the most useful and flexible iAPPs in your arsenal. Whenever someone bothers you (teammates, parents, siblings), put them and you on the WIZ stage and use your wand creatively.

Some you'll want to make disappear, some you'll want to build up and be best friends with. But nobody escapes the WIZ iAPP. Nobody. You might even call yourself an influencer.

24
STOP INTIMIDATION

Engage your inner power to stand up for yourself.

> ❝
> *If you go around being afraid, you're never going to enjoy life. You have only one chance, so you have to enjoy life.*
>
> **— LINDSEY VONN,**
> STAR SKIER ❞

I expect you like being the TECH and using the WIZ iAPP to disappear people from your game, so that it is just you and the target. With practice, you may just be able to believe that the range is your own private club. Now, I'll show you how you can use your WIZ iAPP to become a leader.

One of the benefits of your GO-ZONE is the powerful message you send to your opponents:

"Don't mess with me or my game."

It's written in your posture. In your face. In your willingness to be a loner and isolate yourself from your peers for your 30MR.

In the way you pretend you can't hear them by pointing to your earphones when they try to distract you.

With championships on the line, you need to ignore the drama and keep your socializing where it needs to stay—at the end of the competition. Your game will improve with this kind of focus, along with your ability to practice on your own. And hey, in the long run you'll win way more friends by being a winner.

Be prepared, though, as the road may get rocky at times. You may think others are saying negative things, or trying to isolate you, especially when you start winning. Someone may even let you know that you are being talked about. To stop this from affecting you and your game, you'll need to apply WIZ to help you to sustain your GO-ZONE.

Real-life applications

Each of the following stories is based on true stories of athletes with whom I've worked. They will help you to understand the many ways you can apply WIZ to your game and your life. Since they are all teens, I've altered the names and the stories slightly to protect their identities.

Donnie's Story: Peer pressure

Donnie (not his real name) is a clays athlete who got hooked up with some friends who were vapers. His parents got wind of it and called up Donnie's friends' parents and let them know the situation. Due to the potential consequences (losing his privilege to use the family vehicle), Donnie left his vaping friend group and joined a core group of other friends.

Except, he still had to compete against his former friends as they were always present at competitions. However, he proved herself to be a master TECH and used WIZ to make them "disappear." In his next competition, he stayed in the GO-ZONE and barely even noticed them.

Madison's Story: Coach playing favorites

Madison (not her real name) is a clays athlete. She was on the competitive college team where her coach was playing favorites with a small group of other athletes, mostly her male counterparts. When she asked her coach to check out her technique in preparation for a competition, he spoke to her dismissively.

Over the next few weeks of training, Madison's GO-ZONE turned to a NO-ZONE. Except, Madison started learning to be a great TECH and, armed with WIZ, she imagined herself on her TV screen as a giant as compared to the coach. Immediately, she regained her GO-ZONE and within days her game was back on track.

She also applied WIZ to help her female colleagues overcome the same kind of coach negativity and they worked together as a training group. Both Madison and her training group salvaged the season with great performances.

Emily's Story: The controlling boyfriend

Emily (not her real name) is a clays athlete who had an overly jealous and smothering type of boyfriend. He discouraged Emily from hanging out with her friends and made Emily's friends feel uncomfortable. Her boyfriend even tried to prevent Emily from competing in clays. And, though she persisted, she performed terribly.

Ready to quit the sport, Emily identified her boyfriend's negativity and bullying tactics as the main reason for her poor performances and unhappiness. She empowered herself to be the TECH and used WIZ to help her gain the monster courage to dump him. She did and, with that, reclaimed her GO-ZONE. Not surprisingly, her joy and success in the game she loved returned.

Liam's Story: Extreme shyness

Liam (not his real name) was very, very shy and could hardly make eye contact with anyone. His shooting game in practice was extraordinary but at competitions the shyness kicked in and he lacked confidence on the line.

However, after he learned to be a masterful TECH with WIZ, he became a dominant athlete as an individual and a team leader on his high school team. He also became something of the class clown and, after high school, went on to excel at college. As well as being on the shooting team as the captain, he joined the theater club as one of the lead actors.

Alyssa's Story: Nasty coach

Alyssa (not her real name) is a clays athlete who loves to perform and compete. One day her mom found Alyssa in tears in the restroom. She told her mom that the coach was suddenly being nasty to her and she no longer felt confident with anything.

As you now know the trend with all these case studies, Alyssa was a masterful TECH and, with the help of WIZ, was able to reclaim her GO-ZONE and reduce the impact of the coach. She ultimately left the club, and in her next competition against her old coach's team, she performed well in spite of the presence of the coach.

Be creative...be empowered...be yourself

Wiz is a very powerful iAPP that can be used in every facet of your life, from sport to school, personal relationships to the drama with friends. Just project the other person on a big-screen TV, see your side of the screen and how you are being treated, and tap your wizard wand a few times in the direction of yourself.

Be creative, be empowered, be yourself. By being the TECH and using WIZ, you've just increased your skills and, with practice, installed WIZ as your normal way of dealing with others. And that has got to feel empowering.

There is no Harry Potter magic here, and it may take repeated uses of your WIZ iAPP to resolve how someone treats you. You may have to engage your parents or coaches at times to help you. But this is how you take leadership. And now that you know how to do it, you can reinvent yourself into a champion on the *leader*board.

Skill Drill 24: Manage your relationships

Start noticing how fast WIZ can help you to get over the emotional aspects of the bad or negative behavior of others—just like Donnie, Madison, Emily, Liam and Alyssa did. It may initially take a bit of conscious effort on behalf of your TECH role to place a BP (Bothersome Person) on stage and deal with them, but it will get easier and you'll quickly develop WIZ as a subconscious skill.

In the process, you'll learn to make new, more dynamic and caring friends. Keep your WIZ wand handy (in your back pocket), and pull it out at every opportunity. Because it is your key iAPP for being a leader in your sport and in your life.

Important: If WIZ proves to be ineffective in helping you deal with a bullying or extremely irritating and off-putting individual, seek help from someone in authority (ie, your parents, coaches, teachers or law enforcement officers). Nobody should have to go through this kind of struggle alone.

Next up

In the next chapter, we'll use WIZ one more time to show you how it can be used in school. You'll gain the teacher's trust, learn faster and have more time to train for your next competition.

Training Tip

Make a list of your five top competitors that you'll be competing against in your next competition. If you can see them in your mind, they have beaten you before the competition has even started.

So, one at a time, use your WIZ iAPP to change how you perceive them. On the WIZ screen, build yourself up as dominant and see them as shrinking and beatable. That way, it will be a test of who has the best skills, not who is the most intimidating.

> *If you only ever give 90% in training then you will only ever give 90% when it matters.*
>
> **— MICHAEL OWEN,**
> STAR SOCCER PLAYER

25
UPLEVEL YOUR GPA

Apply high-performance
for success in school.

Magic is believing in yourself.
If you can do that, you can make
anything happen.

— **JOHANN WOLFGANG VON GOETHE,**
Star Poet

It is very empowering to be able to build friendships or disappear distracting people. WIZ is an iAPP that you'll be using for the rest of your life to lead in every role you take on, from your sport to your school to your career. Practice makes perfect. Let's apply that "perfect" to your grades.

In school, even though there are many dynamic teachers, you've likely had a boring one who makes the subject uninteresting and your daydreams even more interesting. Maybe you just feel sleepy. Except you have to stay awake or you'll be down-leveling your GPA.

Just like you overcome the effect of bad officials or referees in clays, you are going to have to overcome a teacher's negative impact, because if that one mark (and that one teacher) affects your GPA and stops you from getting a scholarship, that teacher will likely be a distant memory even as they have had a lasting effect on your future. Now is the time to take action.

Do you know what I did with boring teachers? Exactly. Nothing, because I was ill-equipped and had no strategies. So, by doing nothing I allowed them to affect my marks without even knowing I was allowing them to affect my future.

Now, I can clearly see the impact boring teachers had on me, as all I have to do is compare my poor grades in their classes to one of my excellent classes, where my teacher, (no surprise), was dynamic and engaging. With dynamic teachers I paid attention and did my homework. But with the boring teachers... not so much.

Make every grade count

One of my clients was dealing with a boring professor in college. Steph (not her real name) was studying biology and had taken a genetics class two previous times but had dropped it both times in order to preserve her honors GPA. This third time round was her last chance. I asked her to put a number on the level of her GO-ZONE in Genetics, out of ten.

"Four," she said. "Maybe less."

I asked her if she was a four every time she attended class with that professor.

"Yes," she said, her face tense.

"There is good news and bad news," I said. "The bad news is that as long as you are a four out of 10 in that class, you'll be a four out of ten on your exam.

"The good news is that you have time to change it to a ten out of ten by using the WIZ iAPP and other iAPPs."

Skill Drill 25: The GO-ZONE equals a better GPA

This Skill Drill combines iAPPs to dramatically transform specific grades, as well as transform your perspective of teachers and their perspective of you.

1. **On a piece of paper, draw several boxes, one for each of your subjects this semester.** Write the name of each subject within the box. See the illustration on the next page as an example.

2. **Beside each subject box, put a number (out of 10) that represents your level of GO-ZONE in that subject (10=high passion and 1=low passion).** Steph's subjects would have looked like the following chart in her semester that year:

SUBJECT	ENJOYMENT LEVEL 1 - low | 10 - high
Marine Biology	10 out of 10
Genetics	4 out of 10
Bio Chemistry	9 out of 10
Thesis	9 out of 10
Environmental studies	10 out of 10

3. **Next, start with your lowest scored subject such as Steph's Genetics class.** Imagine that "4 out of 10" level *you* on a giant TV screen, perhaps with a video-game number four floating above your head.

4. **Now select three top high performers in that subject (it could include teachers) and place them beside that *you* on the screen.** Activate your mirror neurons by using the COPYCAT iAPP. Shift the "number 4" (you) into the shoes of the first high performer.
   Notice the shift in your posture and in your GO-ZONE. Repeat COPYCAT with the two other high performers until you can clearly see (and feel) a GO-ZONE shift.

5. **Next, and here is where WIZ comes into serious play, place your current teacher on one side of the screen and you on the other.** Zap yourself into larger-than-life brilliance, until you can see your teacher becoming excited and interested in helping you.

You might be surprised at how easily you can positively influence even your teacher. *Spoiler alert! In no way can you make your teacher disappear like you do your opponents.*

6. **Finish by stepping into the new *"you"* on the screen and take on all the great, empowered and scholarly 10-level ability to your class, your study habits and your dreams.**

7. **And then repeat the exercise** with all remaining subjects that are not where you need or want them to be. (Think scholarship!)

There is no magic to getting good grades, only a combination of your GO-ZONE, COPYCAT and WIZ iAPPs along with paying attention, doing your homework and studying.

You'll get focus from being in your GO-ZONE with the assistance of your WIRED button—and you already know that. You'll get smarts from stepping into the shoes of smart classmates and teachers via your mirror neurons—and you already know that too from COPYCAT. No excuses. You'll get practice by studying and learning from your mistakes with your iGPS. And then you'll fix problems with SNAP, which goes without saying. It's now in your power to elevate your GPA.

Oh and by the way…after graduating with a double major from her college and following this up with a Master's degree, Steph is now a professional in her field of choice—Marine Biology!

Next up

You have completed and installed most of the iAPPs you'll learn in this book, from SNAP to WIZ. In the next chapter, I'm going to introduce you to Step 5, where the system comes together with the iAPP, the Circle of Competition (COC).

Training Tip

In college sports, as part of a school shooting team, clays athletes may have to compete in multiple clays events such as skeet, trap, international skeet, bunker trap, sporting clays and super sporting.

The exercise you used in this chapter can also be used to ensure that each clays discipline is a level-10 GO-ZONE as well. Nothing short of a 10 should be accepted. Nothing. In doing so, you become an influencer of every sport you compete in and, by improving your weakest discipline, you actually improve them all.

TEEN vs TARGET PLAYBOOK

STEP 5

RUN YOUR HIGH-PERFORMANCE SYSTEM

This is where your operating system starts to work automatically as you practice your new tools in everything you do. With it, your game becomes easier, more consistent and more successful.

" *There's no shortcut to success. You have to put in the hours, the days, the weeks, the months, and the years to become a champion.* "

— JIN JONG-OH,
STAR OLYMPIC SHOOTER

26
BE AN ARCHI-TECH

Design continuous improvement in your game.

> *Success is no accident. It is hard work,
> perseverance, learning, studying, sacrifice,
> and most of all, love of what you are doing.*
>
> **— PELÉ,**
> STAR SOCCER PLAYER

You have learned so much in this book already, and I'm guessing that by now you are putting it all together nicely. And if you have lots of competitions ahead, I encourage you to keep training, practicing and reading!

The skills you have learned in this program are designed to help you set your competition goals via your vSELFIE and to go after them by being the TECH to fix the stuff that gets in your way. Emotions—anger, frustration and depression— often result from missed targets, but now you can view these emotions simply as iGPS where you fix them and move on, sometimes in seconds. By doing so, you kick back into that very same GO-ZONE that you unearthed at the start of this book, by being an archaeologist.

When you continually pursue your goals in this manner, you start to refine your GO-ZONE and become better at sustaining it. And because I've now turned so many NO-ZONE athletes into GO-ZONE champions, I've got a pretty good idea of what you now look like on the range—beaming, smiling and standing tall—both in practice and competition.

Even though I'm not working with you directly, I am teaching you to work with yourself. And to do that, you now need to become an architect (Archi-TECH) and understand that your game continuously gets better when you think of it as following the CIRCLE OF COMPETITION (COC).

The COC is not the Circle of Life from the movie *The Lion King*, as no one is going to pass away and appear in billowing clouds overhead. Instead, the COC is going to keep you thriving in your game, competition by competition. It is Step 5 of the system, where every training, every game and every success and failure works to take your game to the stratosphere of success.

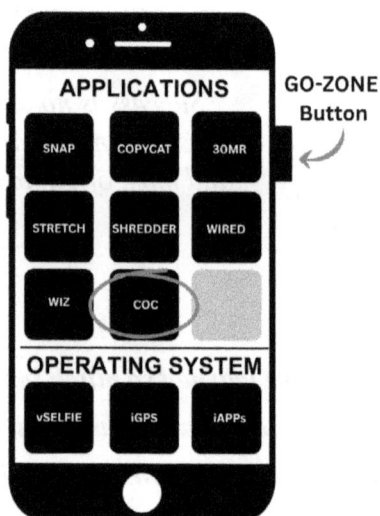

Skill Drill 26: Draw your Circle of Competition (COC)

The circle in the diagram on the next page is your Circle of Competition. It represents the ongoing growth you will experience in competition after competition after competition, in a never-ending upward spiral of success.

1. **First of all, the letters A, B & C in the COC represent key moments in your game.**

   A is the training component, where you *acquire* the skills and strategies and generate the vision (vSELFIE) to be a high performer.

   B is your performance in competition, where you *bring* your GO-ZONE-driven game and discover all the great (and agonizing) iGPS feedback. And **C** is where you continuously debrief and *correct* your competition and throw every iAPP at the wall to see what sticks.

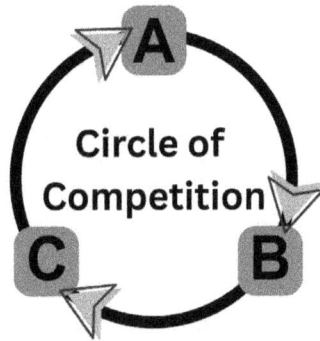

2. **At the A, you set your goals for your next competition.** Here are a few examples:
   - Win!
   - Earn a spot on the team.
   - Get your first 25 straight or clean a station.
   - Have fun.

   You do all the visualizations and skills training so that your GO-ZONE and skills start to feel automatic at a high-performance level.

3. **At B, your competition begins and you perform at your best,** which may feel good and bad at times.

4. **At C, when all is said and done, you review (debrief) your competition** and identify what targets you missed, where you missed them and how you missed them. You become a TECH and use your SNAP iAPP to fix the problems and make corrections. That is one competition down. But are you done? No! The circle continues.

You continue to move around the circle. Back at A, you set new goals such as to win the next competition. You practice all of your strategies, visualizations and skills. At B, you compete again and perform at your best—good, bad or perhaps a little or a whole lot better. At C, the tears have been shed and you debrief your competition and identify what targets you missed, where you missed them and how you missed targets.

This time, as TECH, you use COPYCAT to correct problems with your technique by copying the form of champions you watched at the range. That is two competitions down. You are feeling better and more confident. But are you done? No! The circle continues.

Back again at A, you set new goals and do all the visualizations and training. At B you compete and perform at your best—even better this time! At C, after the nasty stuff has hit the fan, you step into your Archi-TECH role again and use your SHREDDER to deal with the fatigue you felt in your final round. That is now three competitions down and you feel ready to take on the national championship. But are you done? NO! The circle continues.

And you get the idea. You are never done being an Archi-TECH, as you keep moving around the Circle of Competition.

Moving forward (clockwise), from competition to competition, you keep using all of your iAPPs—SHREDDER, WIZ, STRETCH, SNAP. Whether it is for sport, school or personal life, the COC works the same way for each. Your parents will call you resilient! You'll be playing the Archi-TECH and calling it fun!

Be the Archi-TECH to design the COC to drive you forward in this very useful project called *winning*. It will require lots of resiliency, and there can be no whining, complaining or blaming, as all the irritating emotional stuff that pops up in your game is fixable by treating it as iGPS and being a skillful Archi-TECH. The COC is competition and it is life. It is as easy as ABC, but you need to design it so it works for you.

Getting stuck? Ask for help! HELP!

When you get stuck, get bullied or are completely overwhelmed, and your GO-ZONE and iAPPs seem to fail you, ask for help from your parents, your coach or your school teacher. You now have your WIZ to help you to be bold and ask for help. As the saying goes,

"The only stupid question is the one you fail to ask."

And nobody has to act like a know-it-all, because nobody knows it all. The days of coaches putting you down for asking the "stupid" question should be long gone. And so should be those kinds of coaches.

So if someone does make fun of you when you ask your question, trust me on this: That person was probably wanting to ask the same question but they were too afraid to ask. You are the brave one. Go ahead and ask, because even the coach will be grateful that you are helping them to make their point crystal clear.

Next up

The COC never ends as you uplevel your abilities in every area of your life. And do you want to know my biggest regret? Probably not, but I'll tell you anyway. I wish someone had told me about the COC when I was your age. Because I was good at drawing, and even wanted to be an architect at one point. But I never knew I had the power.

So, go for it. You're welcome. And in the next chapter, you'll take the future into your own hands and be a winner.

Training Tip

We often talk about a collapse in a round as going into a downward death spiral where mistakes and misses multiply and our game falls apart.

On the other hand, the COC is a circle that, with improvements, turns into an upward spiral where mistakes get fixed by learning important new skills for better and more consistent results in competitions.

There is no such thing as small stuff, as even the smallest flaw in your technique can turn into multiple lost targets, especially when you get tired or the weather conditions turn against you.

The COC allows you to identify problems (especially the small ones) and fix them before your next cycle of the Circle of Competition.

You *acquire* the tools and practice them to get the job done.
You *bring* your GO-ZONE game.
You continuously *correct* your actions.

It is as easy as ABC.

"

[Competition] forces life to move on.
There's always a new match. A new season.
There's always a dream that everything
can get better. It's a game of wonders.

— FREDRIK BACKMAN,
Star Novelist

"

27
NEVER GIVE UP

Master your game and your future.

> *Never let your head hang down.*
> *Never give up and sit down and grieve.*
> *Find another way.*
>
> **— SATCHEL PAIGE**
> Star Baseball Player

Wow, do you have an incredible toolkit for changing up your game! You have your GO-ZONE to get everything started. You have your vSELFIE of what you want, your iGPS to help you to navigate the rough patches and your iAPPs for paving over them. That is your operating system.

And, as TECH, you can fix any part of your game with the individual iAPPs by themselves or in tandem. With this system, you can (must) use every means to turn adversity into winning results.

For many of you, your competition season has already begun. No matter what level you are at, the Circle of Competition (COC) will work for you. Enjoy it. However, no matter how talented you are, you will fail at times. There are two main responses to failing:

1. You get emotional but use your new strategies to figure it out and get back on track.
2. You get emotional and blame the wind, your squadmates, your parents or your bad luck.

Blaming buries the issue and ensures that you'll repeat mistakes. Taking responsibility and working through the problem will continually improve your game—the COC.

One of the things you'll learn in life is that nobody truly understands the trauma or pain you are going through when you lose, except you. Other people have their own stuff to worry about, and they're just glad that you are the one who is missing targets and not them—so there is no need for you to be embarrassed or in need of sympathy.

And now that you have this program, you know that missing a target is simply iGPS, and it's brilliantly showing you the gaps in your skills and where you need to fix your game. The COC builds a continuous upward spiral by fixing mistakes and skill deficits—round by round, comp by comp—so your winning game grows. With that, who needs sympathy?

Case in point

I watched one of my athletes compete with some good but average rounds in Morocco, North Africa, at a World Cup event. We spoke after the first day to restart his GO-ZONE after the pre-event training went poorly. He could have blamed the pall of dusty air blowing in from the Sahara, or the jet lag or the insane winds, but he smiled and took responsibility.

It was a simple fix. His level of adrenaline had been too calm and as a result, at such a high, competitive level, he missed a couple of targets in a game of perfect, and that was that.

"Nothing is calm about competing,"

I told him.

"We all have to find that perfect level of adrenaline, probably higher than you'd imagine."

So I walked him through SHREDDER. I walked him through COPYCAT. I even walked him through SNAP. And then I signed off and, being late in North Africa, he went to sleep. The next day he scored perfect rounds and finished up the day with a decent score.

Over the next three days he would compete in two team events and win a gold medal in each. And on his return home, he told me that his main iAPP for the team events was WIZ, as it helped him keep his teammates in an adrenalized Zone. And that he did this all by himself by being the TECH.

He followed that performance a month later with a silver medal in Italy and really followed that up a month later with a silver medal at the Olympics in Paris. His name is Conner Prince, Olympian. And he has learned the COC to successfully drive his game.

Skill Drill 27: I've never had a bad competition!

Nobody can force you to care about how you perform. Not your parents. Not your coach. Not your school teachers. Only you can. And the best way to do that is to understand that the person who cares the most about you is you.

Yes, others care. But you have to care more about you than they do, as you build your independence. It won't be long before you are working in your career and fully independent. With the COC, you'll continually improve your game and life skills, and even growing into your new career will be easy.

One of the first things I tell the athletes with whom I work is this: "In three or four months I will ask you one question:"

"Have you ever had a bad competition?"

And then I tell them that I expect the answer to be:

"Well Bob, I must have had a bad competition in order to be as skillful and as successful as I am now, but I can't remember any."

So, even though you have been diligently using your new iAPPs (over these past 26 chapters) to resolve NO-ZONE parts of your game, and even if you believe that you have resolved every last one of them, your task is to search your memory banks for additional NO-ZONE misery! Create a chart, as in the example shown, and do the following exercise:

1. **List past NO-ZONE events in the first column,** whether a single missed shot, a disaster of a round or a whole train wreck of a competition. You can list school and personal events as well. Come up with five or more.
2. **In the second column, put the iAPP you plan to use** to resolve it.
3. **Be the TECH** and fix the problem with that iAPP.
4. **In the final column, note how you feel about each NO-ZONE resolution** and how you believe it will impact your game.

And now, if I ever do meet up with you in person, you'll know the first question I'll ask you, as well as the expected answer. Go to town on it!

NO-ZONE EVENTS	IAPP TO USE TO RESOLVE THE NO-ZONE EVENT	NOTES ON HOW YOU FEEL ABOUT RESOLVING THE NO-ZONE EVENTS
Another competitor intimidated me	WIZ	Can't imagine that person ever bothering me again as they've completely disappeared
The wind affected my game	STRETCH	I feel excited about the next windy event and can't wait to take it on
I felt tired later in the afternoon and didn't shoot as well	SHREDDER	Can't even remember the bad afternoon. Plan to use the SHREDDER shifting next time to stay in the GO-ZONE.
My performance was lousy	SNAP	Can't even remember the bad competition
Hard-right targets cause me to jump at them	COPYCAT	I feel a nice smooth move to the target and the target looks as big as a trash-can lid

Next up

Caring about your game and taking responsibility for your game can be hard work, even with your GO-ZONE, vSELFIE and your iAPPs. Excuses are way easier than rolling up your sleeves and being a TECH, but I'll make you a deal. You take responsibility for your game, and in the next chapter, I'll give you a few of my greatest strategies for winning. See you in the next chapter.

Training Tip

Everyday, use your vSELFIE to fine-tune your game. If you've never been to the range of an upcoming competition, go online to the range's website (with parental permission of course) and get a good overview of the background so that you can include it in your vSELFIE. When you get to the competition, the range should feel like home.

As well, if you have some idea of the weather conditions you'll face for your competition (windy, hot, cold), you can include these into your vSELFIE as well. In this manner, you fine-tune all of these potential elements of your game so that you are as well-prepared as possible.

28
PUT THE FUN BACK IN TRAINING

Test out Bob's three BEST practice strategies.

"

*Excellence is the gradual result
of always striving to do better.*

— **PAT RILEY,**

Star Miami Heat President

"

*With this program, you've been doing a lot of vSELFIES,
staying on track with the COC (Circle of Competition) and using
common-sense iAPPs to stay focused at competitions. I can
imagine that many of you are doing just fine, and I can also
imagine that some of you are still finding staying in the GO-
ZONE to be a challenge.*

*Good or bad, you know what is working for you and what isn't,
which allows you to practice and train smarter.*

You need to build fun in your game in order to avoid becoming
bored with practice. In this chapter, I'll deliver on my top three best
strategies for making your training fun, so you can train smarter.
This goes for school homework as well.

Now, you probably aren't running your own practices, as that is the role of your coach (or mom and/or dad). But you can still adapt your training so that you put time pressure on yourself, include fun challenges such as ever-increasing repetitions of gun mounts and use music to enhance your training. These kinds of training ideas will help you to make practices fun so that you succeed in practice before you even get to the competition.

Skill Drill 28: Incorporate fun into your training

Strategy #1: Time yourself

1. Time your shot process in your practice rounds. This sounds really too simple, but it works. Time everything. Your parents or a squadmate can video your round so that later on you can analyze the video and time your consistency, from your opponent's shot to yours, or from one pair of targets in games like sporting clays to the next. You can watch ISSF (International Sport Shooting Federation) videos of world champions, time the athletes and compare their times to yours. And then you can take this information and apply it to your training sessions so that you fine-tune your process.

2. Time how long it takes to get your vest and gear together. This will help you to see where you get distracted, perhaps by answering texts or talking to your friends, so you can remove these distractions.

3. Time your homework as well. See how long it takes you. But more importantly, see what pops up to distract you.

Text messages from your friends, for example. See where you lose time or focus and eliminate the distraction. By turning off your cell phone (and putting it out of sight), you are going to be more efficient, save time and have more time to do other fun stuff like training.

Plus, you'll be a good role model for your friends. If you feel it's impossible to shut off your cell phone and pull yourself away from your friends for a few minutes, as you might miss an earth-shattering "unfriending," try it out a few times and feel free to blame your coach (Bob) or your parents. Or, you can put an auto-responding message on the text that you are driving your car (toward a podium spot at your next competition).

Strategy #2: Give yourself challenges

1. **This is simple. Challenge yourself in activities to do a certain number of repetitions in a certain period of time.** For example, setting out to do "some" gun mounts will leave you bored and wanting to quit after about five. But doing 50 perfect gun mounts while pretending to be on a range with high adrenaline—that'll get you wired. Keep track of the reps by counting them out loud, and then increase the number of reps next time you do it to keep upping the challenge. Push (by challenging) yourself.

2. **Challenge yourself to stay focused for a limited period of time doing your homework before taking a break and certainly before checking your cell phone (that you left in the other room).** You will quickly

find out what distracts you and can use your iAPPS of SNAP, COPYCAT or SHREDDER to keep eliminating distractions.

This process will start training your mind to extend your ability to focus, which will also help with your practice and competition focus. And by setting this kind of time target, you'll likely get more efficient and get finished in less time and have more time for social activities or practice.

3. **Set yourself up to have no homework, just to see how much you can get done in a short period of time.** My daughter did this by using every spare moment in school to get her homework done. In the midst of her chatting classmates, she stayed super-focused, head down and ploughed through what might have been that night's homework. After school, she used this extra time to train as a swimmer and earn money at her part-time job.

To stay efficient like this, challenge yourself to stay 100-percent focused in school classes with a top-level GO-ZONE. You'd be surprised how much more information you'll retain and how much *less* time you have to spend studying when you get to exam time. Your WIZ iAPP works really well here. You can use it to make your teacher stand out (and be understandable) and make your distracting classmates disappear.

Strategy #3: Listen to music

Listen to music when you train, on the range or when doing gun mounts at home. Pick a playlist that is tuneful and gets you "dancing" through your reps. One of my female hockey players has a pretend dance party before she plays her sport that helps her get wired up for her practices and competitions.

This kind of prep will make training fun, and when other competitors see you totally focused and engaged in your tunes, they'll stay clear and let you have your 30 minutes of undistracted preparation. If they do intrude, you simply point to your earbuds. The message will be clear.

As for music with respect to homework, I remember my daughter always played music in the background. But it is not for everyone and your parents may have set up rules for this. Personally, I needed sound-reducing headphones to keep out the noise of the world when I studied. For me, there is a time for music, but otherwise it is a distraction. That said, I love it thumping away in the background when I'm in the gym training.

This whole chapter is about fun practice, so use these top three strategies to ensure you really, really have fun training. The more you enjoy training, the more training you'll do and the more accomplished you'll become in your sport. Using these strategies will benefit you in your game and every part of your life.

Next up

As you put your plan in place to have more fun in your training, especially as you set out to win, go back and reread previous chapters and review your GO-ZONE, your vSELFIE and your great iAPPS for competition readiness. Make sure you can apply them all, effortlessly.

Many of my athletes have my first book of this series, MIND vs TARGET, plastered with sticky notes and highlighted in yellow, as it is their field guide for using their iAPPs for high performance. Mark this book up too. In the next chapter, I'll take you on a YouTube journey of skill development where you'll get to practice your iAPPs and use them to gain new skills.

Training Tip

Ask your coach for help with this training tip, plus you'll need two other teammates to take part. No equipment is necessary.

1.   Start by getting into your best GO-ZONE.
2.   Then pretend to step into the stand.
3.   Your two teammates are to vocally (no touching) try to distract you and get you to smile. They can tell jokes and poke gentle fun at you.
4.   Your job is to stay focused. If they get you to smile (which is likely), hold up your hand and call a timeout.
5.   In the timeout, take a couple of minutes to be a TECH and use an iAPP (ie. WIZ) to get back to your GO-ZONE. Then you step back in and they try again.
6.   After two timeouts, switch it up and let the others have a try. (Your coach's role is to prevent things from getting crazy.)

"

Don't let them drag you down by rumors,
just go with what you believe in.

— MICHAEL JORDAN

"

29
CONSUME A GOOD SOCIAL-MEDIA DIET

Build your skills with wise viewing choices.

"

Your biggest opponent isn't your opponent.
It's human nature.
[And what you may read about yourself on social
media - Bob's editorial addition.]

— **BOBBY KNIGHT,**
Star Coach

"

With what you are learning and applying here, I'm imagining
that you are having fun and building your success in practices
and in competitions. Whether you are just starting your season,
or you're in full swing, or your championships are around the
corner, keep doing your vSELFIEs with full adrenaline and
brilliant "unrealistic" outcomes, because you need to feel your
intense GO-ZONE at competitions even before the targets fly.

Many years ago, prior to social media being invented, I was flying
for the first time ever enroute to my first teaching job in Northern
Canada. From my jet window the Canadian geography rolled out
ahead of me, something that I'd only ever seen via maps, air photos

and ground travel. Now I was seeing it with my own eyes from the bird's-eye view. On this cloudless day, the absolute beauty of it blew me away.

Today, you can call up Google Maps and fly anywhere you want and see what I saw—on demand. This is your new reality—without the need for the plane. This is normal for you, as you are a member of the very first generation to have (and be in control of) all the visual content of the world. Not only Google Earth, everything! Namely the good and bad of YouTube, Instagram, TikTok and all of social media.

What you watch can help or hurt your game

With your cell phone, you have a high-pressure fire hose of information in your hands that you can use to propel yourself to the top of your game. But you'll need to be selective, as the information fire hose can be intense. Why? Because your mirror neurons are running in the background taking everything in, both the good and bad of everything you watch.

So, let's talk about how to control your social media diet in order to protect your mirror neurons, so you can become a student of the game and keep getting more skillful. It will be similar to going on a food diet. You already know how beneficial it is for your high-performance game to eat healthy. In this case, you'll want to watch only the empowering videos that feed your mirror neurons a healthy diet of the skills and strategies of high performers and champions.

In Chapter 12 you learned the COPYCAT iAPP as a strategy to improve your skills by specifically stepping into the shoes of champions. At the speed of light, you harnessed your mirror neurons and copied multiple new skills.

But I warned you then that mirror neurons can be dangerous as they are always running and always searching for someone to copy—such as bad form or even bad attitudes. With that in mind, here's a plan to improve your game by watching only the good stuff on social media.

Skill Drill 29: Create a game plan for social media

Skill Drill 29 is based on you following your parents' rules and having parental permission to use social media. If you have their permission, fire up your social media and have some fun learning from experts.

1. **Create a specific plan before you grab your cell phone to access your social media.** Your plan may be to become more skillful in a specific component of your sport, such as gun mounts or move to the target or researching and modeling specific career options such as becoming a doctor, vet, technician, military personnel or musician.

    Or you can learn the physiology of staying in the Zone during a specific part of your event. Or you can relax by watching funny animal videos.

    Your plan should also include a screen-time time limit (20 minutes or less), so set your timer as it will help you be more specific as it will serve as a constant reminder that this is a mission, not mindless entertainment. You want to avoid getting sucked into the endless void of reels that are professionally designed to be addictive.

2. **Pick a topic for your plan such as "Seeing the clay target better" and then do the search.** My top two YouTube search picks for that search were coaches whom I just happened to know. They are respected coaches and work with both beginners and Olympians. So YouTube got it right. The next videos on the list posted by YouTube looked interesting as well, though I did not know these coaches.

3. **Trust your GO-ZONE.** You'll know immediately if the trainer is in their GO-ZONE or not, as you'll naturally find the videos interesting. Your adrenaline level should increase as your mirror neurons copy their physiology (posture and skills). If the video falls flat, search for another video with a more dynamic coach.

4. **Stay on topic.** Become an expert skipper of videos that, although interesting and vying for your attention, are off-topic and sometimes seem to be deliberately getting you into the NO-ZONE. With my search, a couple of distractions came up regarding planting gardens in clay soil and turning clay pots on a potter's wheel.

5. **Shut off YouTube after the time limit, and spend some time using your COPYCAT iAPP to step into the shoes of the presenter.** COPYCAT will tell you how much in

the GO-ZONE they were, as well as teach you some impressive new skills, most of which you won't even know you are learning.

6. **Go test what you just learned on the range from your social media practice sessions.** How you perform in your next training practice on the range will tell you how well you exercised your mirror neurons. But keep them on a short leash, for, as you know, they vacuum up everything, good and bad.

With this approach, the world of social media and learning is in your hands—and when used properly, it can be a truly amazingly-controlled fire hose of information that can propel you to the podium. Visit social media sites for a diet of "healthy" social media and then be the TECH to use COPYCAT to specifically "install" the skills that you watched. Your GO-ZONE will give you feedback on how healthy the social media diet was.

When you feel your GO-ZONE become stronger, great. When it feels diminished, press the skip button and move on or turn off your device and go for a run, hit the gym, do homework or call up (rather than text) a friend. Trust what you feel.

Next up

Generate more fun in your training by learning great new ways of training and great new approaches to the techniques of your game. You have an abundance of information that you can access and may have already accessed through your cell phone.

Now, go back and reread and review all the iAPPs in this book. Use them to challenge every aspect of your training. Embed them in how you behave on and off the range. Truly make them a part of the upward growth spiral of the COC, your Circle of Competition.

And then, in the next chapter, you'll launch your game into the stratosphere with Step 6, adding new roles of Innovator and CEO. You will design new ways to train, take a new look at leadership and learn to trust your abilities.

Training Tip

1. Create your own YouTube instructional video. Set up your phone so that it covers one stand at the range (or a pretend stand in your rec room).

Introduce yourself and describe what you are going to do, such as,

"I'm now going to demonstrate what the GO-ZONE looks like and how to use it in the stand."

2. Then, get into your best GO-ZONE physiology, step into the stand and execute the shot.

3. After the shot, step out and say something about it.

"You may notice that my posture was upright and that made me feel so good I couldn't miss. That is the kind of GO-ZONE I use on every shot."

4. Finally, when you get it right, show the video to your coach or parents and ask them what they think of your GO-ZONE (and video making).

"

Nothing will work unless you do.

— JOHN WOODEN
Star Basketball Coach

"

TEEN vs TARGET PLAYBOOK

STEP 6

STRIVE FOR EXCELLENCE

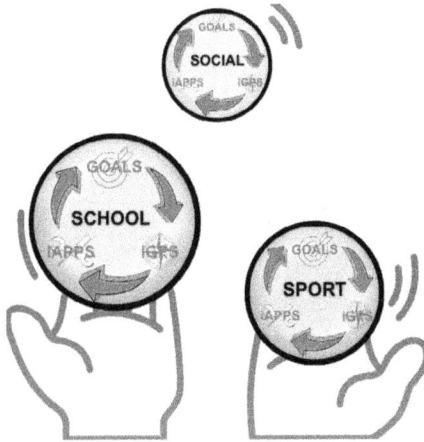

This is where you step back and see the big picture and juggle all aspects of your sport, school and social life. You take leadership, build relationships, act creatively and trust in your abilities as you apply your passion to your sport and life.

"
*I was told over and over again that
I would never be successful, that I was not going
to be competitive and the [Fosbury]
Technique was simply not going to work.
All I could do was shrug and say,
'We'll just have to see.'*

— DICK FOSBURY
STAR HIGH JUMP INNOVATOR
"

30
INNOVATE YOUR GAME

*Create new ways to test out and improve your
performance.*

> "
> *If you don't try things and take risks,
> you don't really grow and figure out
> what you want.*
>
> **— ZENDAYA,**
> STAR SINGER
> "

*You have now built your system for high performance, even
going so far as to copy the skills of the champions that you've
researched on social-media sites. You have an incredible
program for excellence and are following in the footsteps of
many champions. You have learned how to ignite your GO-
ZONE, how to utilize your "operating system" (Goals, GPS and
iApps) and how to apply your new iAPPs to resolve just about
any challenge.*

*But there is no stopping now. In order to be a champion, you
need to be a creator, as following the pathway to winning often
requires that you display a great deal of innovation to rise to the
podium.*

You have now arrived at the last step, Step 6, where you will be taking charge of your game. I would never have won anything or have become a trainer of Olympians if I'd accepted everything I was told and acted like a mindless sheep. I took charge of my own destiny. I owned it. It was all about me.

When things failed to work for me, I changed them up. When books told me to take deep breaths and relax when I was nervous, and all that did was make me more nervous, I went down in my basement and figured it out. I added crazy adrenaline to that nervous scaredness and screamed karate yells as I worked on my vSELFIE. In the process I developed WIRED.

Only then did I feel the true impact of an adrenalized and tsunami-like wave of my GO-ZONE for the first time. Only then did I realize that someone else's advice had been wrong and only I could have corrected it!

This is how I learned to win—by questioning what I was told, questioning my weaknesses and being innovative until I got it right. It is how all top athletes learn and adapt what their coaches, their parents and the adversity of the game teaches them, so that small changes to their training bring really big changes to performance.

With this kind of iGPS, within the always improving COC, your game evolves as you learn to win, which truly is the main reason why you play the clays game in the first place.

Skill Drill 30: The advantages of being a creator and an innovator

You are going to act like a creator, where you will use your creativity to continually level up your training program to gain an edge on your competition. As a creator, you'll need to constantly test new ways to practice, sometimes with your coach and sometimes without.

Initially your coach will know way more than you. But as you grow and develop, you may be the best person to figure out (by using the tools in this program and what your coaches have taught you already) what is frustrating you or holding your back. And then you figure out how to fix it, often through experimentation and creativity.

The list that follows is your starting list. I say "starting list," because your innovations will be closely tied to your own game, not mine and not anyone else's. Creators like you get over the bumps and humps in your road so that you can strive for your podium success.

Your list should also have a high likelihood of failure, so that you can work with your iAPPs to improve. Be the creator and fix the gaps in your skills! Take the lead.

Over the next weeks and months of training, invent games or activities that:

1. **Create stresses that force you to overcome game-like situations.** Example: *You must shoot a round perfectly or start over.*

2. **Help you connect better with the target ("by pretending to be the target").** Example: *Find an unused range and walk or run (or pretend to fly) all the potential target trajectories for each stand.*

3. **Get to peak energy level quickly.** Example: *Set a special alarm for earlier than usual in the morning and see how fast you can get into the GO-ZONE, step into an imagined stand and call pull.*

4. **Raise or lower your adrenaline so you can learn to manage it.** Example: *When hanging with boring friends, see how long it takes you to get them in the GO-ZONE by regulating your adrenaline.*

5. **Generate fatigue or exhaustion that forces you to resolve it.** Example: *Do a hundred pushups, run several miles and then, after only a few minutes to collect yourself, get into your GO-ZONE, step into a stand and shoot a round. Or: Shoot a round with a distracting pebble in your shoe.*

6. **Pit yourself against your training partners where they play by the same weird rules.** Example: *Everyone deliberately alternates the timing of their shot process, one time very slow and one time very fast, in an attempt to be distracting.*

7. **Ensure flexibility and support your GO-ZONE.** Example: *Borrow an opposite-handed shotgun and teach yourself to shoot with the other hand from scratch, without losing your GO-ZONE.*

Now I made up these examples in about five minutes, but every one of these games will move you forward in some component of your game. And, just as this book is the result of years of me challenging the strategies and ideas that made no sense and overcoming the blocks that worked against me, your game will improve with each new invention, especially when you apply your iAPPs to deal with various blocks in your game.

You are at the beginning of writing your own story, your own book, your own self-coaching manual. Step outside of your so-called comfort zone and invent new approaches to training that will take you to the top of the leaderboard.

Up Next

In the next chapter, we'll play just one more role, that of being a leader or a CEO, where you are the talent, and your coaches, parents and all others are a part of your team. As CEO, you take the initiative.

Be a creator and invent a game to help you train better and video record it. It might be something you create next week, next month or even next year. No rush. I just want you to start thinking like a creator.

Training Tip

The game needs to have a purpose such as inducing competition-like stress. It has to be something you can do by yourself, such as spotting a less skillful player a couple of extra birds and forcing yourself to be perfect in order to beat them. And it has to be useful to others as they watch your video.

31
BE A LEADER-IN-TRAINING

Understand the roles of your support team.

> *If you want to go fast, go alone.*
> *If you want to go far, go together.*
>
> **— AFRICAN PROVERB**

You have played many roles thus far in this book and I hope that you are enjoying the process, perhaps even earning an imaginary Oscar for each role! Playing roles never really stops, as you'll take on so many in your life in the future. But I've got one more for you.

To enhance and round out the skills of your game, you are going to take on one of your most important roles to date, that of being the pretend CEO of your *team*. You have the skills; you have the support from parents and coaches; and you have the product (you). It's time to take leadership and pull the team together.

In this pretend role of CEO, you'll gain insights into how your parents think and make decisions, understand the financial stresses they may be under and plan how to make their and your job easier, perhaps by taking on greater responsibility.

With this approach, you'll learn the importance of communication and setting up team meetings with your parents and coaches in order to make this a truly awesome experience. What you'll learn about leadership will benefit you now and in the future.

Become the iCEO of your "team"

I developed the imaginary CEO (iCEO) role to prepare my professional athletes for their post careers, as most cannot even imagine a future beyond sport. It brings up a lot of fear, and most won't even talk about it.

But, by imagining themselves as iCEOs, right now, where their athletic ability is the product, they put in place a business structure where their coaches, agents, financial advisors and sponsors are a part of their "team."

With this team structure, they run their sport like a business, and, when retirement eventually comes, these sport/business professionals simply exchange themselves as the product for another product, such as representing clothing lines or selling yachts or investing in real estate.

And guess what? I've found this to be a very empowering model for all of my athletes, at all ages and all levels. While you

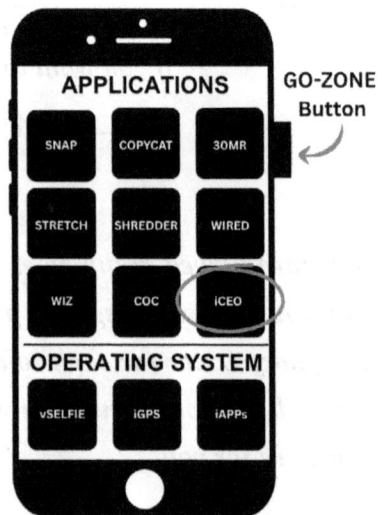

may not be an Olympian or pro, and may be just starting your competitive career, thinking of yourself as an iCEO of your team is the most important thing you can do to make you (and your team) a winner.

As an iCEO, you will be tasked with staying in your GO-ZONE to keep your team happy and in their GO-ZONE—the coaches (technical and high performance), the banker (your parents), the chauffeur (your parents), the manager (your parents), the chef (your parents), yourself (the skilled athlete), your teammates (your cheerleaders) and your competitors (the impressed). As iCEO, this is the imaginary team you will guide.

Your role as the "product"

You are the reason your iCEO exists—as you are the product. It's your amazing skill, passion and your determination. It's your ability to learn and apply technical skills from your coach and high-performance skills from a high-performance trainer.

And it's your ability to enhance yourself as the product by your commitment to school and college. Without a product, there's no business and a limited future. With a great product, the sky's the limit at the level you are playing at and beyond.

What's your passionate goal and how does that look as a vSELFIE?

How hard are you willing to work in practice to refine your skills as the product?

This allows you to put some nice, extra pressure on yourself to perform.

Your parents' roles on your team

Your parents (or maybe a grandparent, relative or mentor) are the foundation of your team. Without them, there would be no team and no potential for excelling in your sport. Athletes with whom I've worked often forget this, mostly because parents act like parents—driving, paying the bills, cooking meals, scheduling and lugging equipment. And this is only the start of the list.

Unbeknownst to most athletes, parents may be stressed about finances, taking time off work for your competitions and managing paying off hotel and entry fees, while giving up their own activities, a sacrifice they make because they believe in you.

And when athletes like you are very talented and require top-of-the-line equipment and coaching, or high-performance training from someone like me, the pressure is even greater and the cost can be huge. When you start to see your parents in this light, they likely need the front seat on your imaginary team, not the back one.

So, thinking of your parents as your banker, chauffeur, cook and advisor for your business, along with any other roles they fill, it gives you, the iCEO, more incentive to work your tail off to make sure that their investment is solid. And for their other roles, they get the occasional thank you. Thank you!

This new insight about your parents, may also give you incentive to pick up a part-time job (such as coaching), calling companies to inquire about sponsorships or getting your driver's license so that you share in chauffeuring.

You will find that by keeping your parents (in all of their roles) in the loop (by talking to them), you'll be able to demonstrate how their investment is paying off and why they should keep you well funded and around. It will also show them your character and the great human being and citizen they are guiding you to become.

The coach's role on your team

You typically think about a coach as helping you to become more skillful, guiding you to stay on track, softening the blow of crushing defeats and holding you accountable, often through encouragement, guilt and/or disciplinary action. Pretty straightforward. But when you are an iCEO, you'll need to think of your coach differently, perhaps as your consultant, where you hold each other accountable.

That means going to every practice in your GO-ZONE and being prepared to train hard, while at the same time expecting your coach to be in their GO-ZONE as well. And if they are not, you use your WIZ iAPP to train your coach to be more GO-ZONE-like. A better practice will be the result, the relationship will be stronger, and you'll learn much, much more from them.

Your teammates' and competitors' roles on your team

Your teammates and competitors are a part of your team as well, because high-performance teammates and competitors push you to be more competitive by becoming more skillful, and vice versa, as you push them.

At the end of the day, after you compete with them, they often become your best friends. Without competitors, there is no game. With no game, you have no reason to improve. Keep your teammates happy and your competitors friendly.

Skill Drill 31: Develop into a skillful leader of your "team"

In this drill you are going to set yourself up for leadership success with your iCEO. All leaders have clearly observable qualities and we are going to copy their attributes.

1. **In your role as iCEO, develop into a skillful leader.** Your role models are everywhere: your parents, key teachers at school, upstanding members of the community, social-group leaders, youth volunteer leaders, Scout leaders, 4-H leaders and pastors.

   If not, look to the internet and expand your social-media diet beyond just watching videos of basic skills to watching videos showcasing military leaders talking about the tactics of navy SEALS or sports coaches talking about motivational strategies that helped them to win.

2. **Create a list of leadership attributes you'd like to gain.** To get you started, I've provided you with some examples:
   1. Good communicator
   2. Passionate

3. Empathetic

4. Holds others accountable

5. Disciplinarian in a firm but empowering way

6. Empowering

7. Tells good stories

8. Organized

9. Good time manager.

3. **Now, use your COPYCAT iAPP to "install" these attributes into yourself for the given roles you play.** Look at yourself in the mirror while doing this exercise so that you can observe postural changes and the expression on your face, as you model various individuals.

4. **And then imagine giving the motivational "talk" to your team.**

At this point, until you test out your new skills, you may not even know what you have just learned. Some vSELFIE practice will help for sure, but ultimately you have to take on a leadership role and lead.

Lead, lead, lead.

And if you fail (and you will), your role models and mentors are always right beside you, offering all the leadership skills in the world—only mirror neurons away.

Next up

Now that we have all of your business roles identified and your iCEO skills have been updated through the modeling process, in the next chapter we'll set you up as iCEO of your family team, where you empower everyone to be in the GO-ZONE. You get to reimagine your clays game as a business run by you, the iCEO. Take charge and win.

Training Tip

Find someone in a leadership role and ask if you can spend a day at work shadowing (observing) them. It might be one of your parents, a family member, a neighbor or the parent of a friend.

Spend the day observing what it is like to be a leader. It can be fun and I guarantee it will activate your mirror neurons big time. I can also guarantee that most leaders will be pleased that you'd even ask.

32
TEST YOUR LEADERSHIP

*Challenge and empower yourself and
your support team.*

"

*Talent wins games, but teamwork and
intelligence win championships.*

— MICHAEL JORDAN,
STAR BASKETBALL LEADER

"

*On top of your GO-ZONE, your Operating System and your
multiple iAPPs, you will now install another iAPP for leadership
of your team. Now that you have identified and started to model
the leadership attributes that will drive your team, you will need
to build the structure for your team in order to strengthen all
aspects of your team's performance.*

Of the many thousands of athletes I've worked with, most take on
leadership roles. Leadership is a normal part of their striving to
get to the top of the *leader*board, so it is not surprising that they
thrive on *leader*ship roles in their sport or other areas of their life,
such as:

High school or college team captain.
Assistant coach on a football team.
Founder of a shooting club.
Volunteer coach of 4-H and high school teams.
Founder of a start-up, grass-cutting business.
Military cadet leader.

Very likely, with your sport and existing leadership roles, you are engaged in some level of leadership and fit the model of most of my athletes. If you are not, I suggest you start.

Do everything in your power to step into leadership roles, even if you are scared to do so and have no idea what you would do as a leader.

Build experience by attending youth leadership groups and summer leadership camps. Find leadership experiences that, ultimately, are going to give you a foundation for your leadership roles in the future, in sport, business and life.

Skill Drill 32: Build and empower your team

Whenever you take on a leadership role, unrelated to your role of picking up a shotgun and crushing clays, it forces you to step outside of your comfort zone. Excitingly, this discomfort is a parallel pathway to the discomfort of the blocks that get in the way of being number one on the leaderboard. So, leadership is leadership.

So, let's do a practice run at leadership and apply the attributes you learned in the previous chapter to your role of iCEO, and in doing so, apply it to all of the roles you identified as being members of your team.

Draw up a team diagram similar to the one in the example shown and insert your own roles:

1. **On a sheet of paper, draw an oval surrounded by circles, as in the diagram.**

2. **Fill in your role of iCEO and product, as well as those of your team, similar to the diagram.**

3. **Use your WIZ iAPP to uplevel and improve your iCEO relationship with all members of your team.** The goal is to empower them. (Interestingly, you can also use this approach with your role as "product" and empower yourself.)

With WIZ, imagine yourself with each member of your team on the WIZ "screen," one at a time. You'll be looking to wave your wand and transform your physiology in your iCEO role, with improved posture and a smile on *your* face. You will especially be firing up your GO-ZONE, as you imagine each team member taking a turn on the stage. Finally, the powerful GO-ZONE shift that you are imagining in yourself, as iCEO, should be having an impact on your team members—their empowered images smiling and drawn into your contagious GO-ZONE, via their mirror neurons.

4. **Now that you have done the leadership work, when the time is right, set up meetings with each member of your team** (excluding your opponents of course), and discuss your goals for your season and beyond.

When you sit down with your coaches, "bankers" and teammates and discuss the "business," you will likely get feedback on the product (you), and you will be able to discuss your goals and dreams for the coming year, both for sport and school.

Most importantly, these meetings are a unique opportunity for giving your "bankers" a heads-up for your future needs of equipment and travel budgets, so that finances can be planned, a game plan drawn up, and alternative sources of funding can be acquired (sponsors, part-time job, etc.).

Maybe you'll get too much information at times in these meetings, or maybe none at all. But you'll start learning about budgeting, finance, communication, negotiation and setting training goals. You will gain a whole new appreciation of the commitment your team makes toward your success, especially the bankers!

Plus, you'll learn to make decisions on getting your product to market (also known as getting on the podium or acquiring a scholarship). And the bonus is that, like my pro athletes, you will be able to apply your iCEO role to all future business endeavors beyond sport.

Being an iCEO can be a challenging job

So, what do you do if after all of this hard work of setting yourself as the iCEO, you find that you are the only one on a team who seems to care about putting in the work? What if your parents are too busy making a living or helping your other siblings? What if your coaches have a hundred other athletes and you are just a number? What if your teammates just want to socialize, and thereby give you no competition in training sessions? The answer is:

You simply take leadership.

Before one of my athletes accepted a college scholarship, I scouted the team for him by using COPYCAT. I stepped into the coach's (and all of the players) shoes, and it was bad news. The coach and players were NO-ZONE all the way.

I warned my athlete of this potential challenge, but he accepted the scholarship anyway. Why? Because over his previous four years of high school he'd led his team to several championships. Now, he was more than prepared to accept that same responsibility at college. And he did it in spades! How? He simply took leadership.

So, now you know... when you care passionately about winning, you have to be the one to take the iCEO role seriously. Your GO-ZONE becomes the model for that passion for everyone on your team. Your job as iCEO is to figure out a way to make it happen.

Next up

I can tell you right now, when you take on the role of iCEO and meet with the members of your team, it will blow them away. It will be one of your most memorable and powerful roles where others will take you seriously.

And in the next chapter, as you likely have competitions around the corner, we'll look at the one final and major skill for you to accomplish—that of taking yourself seriously by simply trusting your abilities and taking leadership of yourself.

Training Tip

One of the things you'll notice by being an iCEO is that you will think differently about everything, from your training to the equipment you use, from your dependence on your parents to your efforts at being independent, from your willingness to be a follower to your efforts to lead. Most importantly, CEOs think long-term.

So, when you have a moment, I'd like you to create a list of your long-term iCEO goals, such as how many sponsors you'll have and who they'll be, what your "coaching" staff will look like and the ROI (Return On Investment) by your parent-bankers such as you getting a scholarship or winning prize money. Keep it a fun exercise, "seriously" fun.

33
TRUST YOUR ABILITY

Stop thinking and shine.

"

Adversity causes some athletes to break;
others to break records.

— **WILLIAM A. WARD,**
STAR MOTIVATOR

"

You, the iCEO, have been working hard on your sport business. With your GO-ZONE, your operating system (vSELFIE, iGPS, iTOOLs) and a really fabulous iAPP toolkit, I expect that you are now doing really well in your game and in school. You are the TECH with the ability to fix all parts of your game—so that you have way more fun and win. It's up to you to get out there and show what you can do.

There is one more thing that I need to prepare you for. Once you have your game (technical) skills and your performance (mental) skills in place, you have to stop thinking of these skills and just pull the trigger.

In the GO-ZONE.
No thinking.

And that is what you're going to learn here, because when you learn to trust your abilities and stop thinking, it will lead to some pretty significant improvements in consistency.

Learn to stop thinking

In the martial art of karate, I competed in point fighting, where combatants fight each other with controlled techniques to score points, not to inflict (much) pain. Most kicks and punches are fast and furious but pulled an inch shy of making full contact, although some (many) can be overaggressive.

In a typical flurry of sparring, I understood that I needed to be able to block automatically, without worrying about incoming strikes or potential pain. This reflexive response to attacks had to be as automatic as riding a bike where I peddled, steered and remained upright without thinking. Truly, if I saw a strike coming at me, it was likely too late for me to block it.

I'd previously experienced plenty of times of fast, non-thinking reflexes, so I knew I had it in me and I knew I had to make that reflexive response normal. So in a training session, I put a plan in place where I would go "full in" to battle without consciously blocking attacks.

In the first fight, I sidestepped attacks and countered with my own strikes, while avoiding overaggressive and sometimes painful hits, all the while deliberately refusing to block. It hurt to not block. A lot. I dodged and weaved and threw valiant counterstrikes, but threw not even one block.

A funny thing happened in my second fight (besides the not-so-funny bruising). I sensed an internal kind of NO-ZONE anger in my core, as though my subconscious mind was getting cross at the ridiculousness of what I was doing.

In my third fight, with my continued refusal to block (and a lot more bruising, as it seemed my colleagues sensed my vulnerability), that NO-ZONE feeling dropped down into my gut and really started to churn.

By about the fifth fight, the anger was purely volcanic.

By the tenth, it spewed forth with a flurry of lava-like adrenaline with blocks and effective well-delivered, well-controlled strikes on my opponent. It was aggressive, a non-thinking explosion of pure passion.

I laughed out loud at that moment. I celebrated. I knew that I would never have to (consciously) block again. My subconscious mind and conscious mind had come to an agreement.

Develop subconscious performance

As a clays shooter, through conscious drills, you've trained your techniques to be routine and automatic. You've practiced gunmounts many, many thousands of times, and done innumerable vSELFIEs to support them. Now, you need to stop thinking after your pre-shot routine, and let your subconscious mind do what you trained it to do.

It is an agreement between your conscious mind and your subconscious mind. The conscious mind does the setup. The subconscious mind moves to the target, pulls the trigger and the target is dust.

Skill drill 32: Trust your subconscious mind to perform

One way that you can get to that agreement is by distracting your conscious mind by getting it to think about something else—such as a swimming breaststroke. It can be a bit unnerving at first, but implementing a breaststroke visualization acts in the same way that a spam filter screens out junk mail. Only you'll be screening out junk thinking (self-talk), the kind of thinking that interferes with your successful, smooth, GO-ZONE move to the target.

So, let's hand over the task of crushing the target to your subconscious mind. It's pretty amazing, really. Trust that your subconscious mind can do what it is really, really good at: crushing clays.

1. **Be ready and fully adrenalized via WIRED.**
2. **Set your eyes into peripheral-vision mode.** To do this, look out a window at a distant object, such as a tree. Place your two index fingers in front of you at arms length. Stare through them toward the object. Now, move your fingers (still at arm's length) around to the sides of your head. You should now see the object in front and your fingers to your sides, in a full 180 degrees or more of your vision. This is peripheral-vision mode.
3. **Notice your heightened awareness.** Notice your mind is quiet with no self-talk. Your eyes must remain in peripheral-vision mode for the remainder of this exercise.
4. **Start moving your arms in a swimming breast stroke motion, with actual physical arm movements.** Do this pretend-swimming motion for several minutes to get fully immersed in the physical movement. With your eyes in

peripheral-vision mode, track your hands outwards and back to the center, as you "swim." The intensity of your adrenaline at this point needs to be very high.

5. **Now, pretend to hold your shotgun, with the breast-stroking movements only a visualization, and your eyes still in peripheral mode,** and step into an imaginary stand.

6. **While continuing to do the breast stroke as a visualization, initiate your pre-shot routine, and call pull.** The breaststroke acts like a spam filter to your conscious mind, allowing the subconscious mind to track the imaginary target, pull the trigger and complete the breaking of the target—without any thinking. All you do is call pull.

7. **Repeat this several times, shooting an entire stand, a complete round or a complete course.** You've been training your subconscious mind for this moment—to track and crush the clay target without thinking. Once you feel comfortable with this exercise, and can sustain your eyes in peripheral mode, test this out at the range.

A word of caution here. You'll have to practice this exercise many times as a visualization (*v*SELFIE) in the distraction-free environment of your home, before you ever attempt to take it on the range. And for those of you who do other more physical sports, you will *only* do this as a *v*SELFIE, as it would be too risky to attempt to do it during a physically-active game such as hockey or gymnastics. But, technically, the application is the same.

A word of advice, too. When you train with others you will (likely) get competitive and give up on trying something new such as this exercise, as initially it may result in you missing and looking silly (as I must have looked when I was incompetently blocking my opponents). So, train alone if you can, and you'll fully gain the benefits of this exercise and other training exercises you use.

Next up

From here on in, high performance is all about you. Put these tools into practice and you'll have fun succeeding in anything to do, as you now have a complete system for winning in your sport and in your life.

From your GO-ZONE and your operating system of your *v*SELFIE, iGPS and iAPPs, to a stellar collection of internal applications that you now own, I've launched you. And in the next chapter, I give you the final quiz to see if you are up for the challenge of taking your game to the podium.

Training Tip

In every practice, you can (must) train in three phases:

First phase: Break everything down into its component parts. For every technique or move to the target, that could be 5 to 10 steps that you carefully think about and follow.

Second phase: Reduce the number of steps by half and think about each step and feel the better flow in your technique.

Third phase: Reduce the number of steps to just one, where you trust your skills and call pull.

Repeat: In each practice, repeat this three-phase process to build total trust in your game. Once you *get it*, the swimming breaststroke is optional!

"

Fans don't boo nobodies.

— REGGIE JACKSON
STAR BASEBALL PITCHER

"

34
PUT YOUR KNOWLEDGE ON THE LINE

Take the quiz!

"

It's not the will to win that matters.
It is the will to prepare to win that matters.

— PAUL "BEAR" BRYANT,
STAR COACH

"

With any program, there always needs to be some way of testing how you are doing. In your game, the real test is how you apply the program I've presented to you on the range. My guess is that by implementing these tools, you are already seeing huge improvements in your game. So, in this chapter and for the fun of it, I've provided a written quiz, because every good training program tests your ability. I think you'll enjoy it.

For many of you, you are now more knowledgeable about high performance, the GO-ZONE and the fact that you have an operating system, than most professional athletes. So, this quiz is for fun and a review, not meant as an examination. Once you have read the book and practiced the exercises in the program, the answers will be pretty easy.

Skill Drill 34: Questions

There are really no wrong answers, as I hope the ones you get incorrect will simply be iGPS feedback and have you running back to re-read specific chapters and figure them out. The answers are noted below this quiz.

1. **What is my GO-ZONE?**
   a. A place where construction takes place.
   b. My bedroom.
   c. A personal, internal sensation that tells me that I am ready to compete.
   d. A flower garden.

2. **If I have limited competition experience, what is the best way to get way more experience in the shortest amount of time?**
   a. Compete 12 hours a day, every weekday, weekend, even in the winter.
   b. Visualize every day with full adrenaline.
   c. Play video games.
   d. Clean my equipment.

3. **What is iGPS in this program and what is the benefit of it?**
   a. A metaphor for letting my mistakes and losses guide me back on track.
   b. Letters of the alphabet.
   c. School grades.
   d. An awful sickness.

4. **What is the benefit of being a TECH in my sport?**
   a. I can get an apprenticeship.
   b. I can fix my bike and ride to practice.
   c. I can help mom or dad download computer files of registration forms.
   d. I can think like a TECH and use my iAPPs to fix my game.

5. **Why is being forgetful a real asset when I compete?**
   a. Mom or dad will look after any equipment I leave behind.
   b. I quickly forget catastrophes and can move on fast.
   c. I can forget to practice and save on shells.
   d. I can forget to do my homework and train more.

6. **If I use SNAP, what am I doing?**
   a. Irritating my friend sitting in front of me.
   b. Clearing away cookie crumbs.
   c. Forgetting a dismal performance.
   d. Playing center in football.

7. **If I want to be as skillful as my role model, what is the best iAPP to use?**
   a. SNAP.
   b. SHREDDER.
   c. POOL GUY.
   d. COPYCAT.

8. **If I want to see the target as bigger and slower, what iAPP might I use?**
   a. LENS CLEANER.
   b. STRETCH.
   c. SHREDDER.
   d. BE GONE.

9. **I'm terrible with presentations at school. What iAPP might I use?**
   a. QUIT SCHOOL.
   b. WIZ.
   c. SHREDDER SHUFFLE.
   d. CHEAT SHEET.

10. **I lose focus during rounds and miss easy targets. What could I do?**
    a. Set my alarm clock.
    b. Put an irritating pebble in my shoe.
    c. Have my mom or dad shout at me.
    d. Increase my level of adrenaline by being an engineer.

11. **I'm being bullied and teased by older athletes on the team. What could I do?**
    a. Tell a parent.
    b. Use WIZ.
    c. Hang around with teammates who make me feel good.
    d. All of the above.

12. **Why do competitions help me become better at clays?**

   a. They push me to figure things out.

   b. I become more creative.

   c. I work harder on my training because I like to win.

   d. All of the above.

13. **What is the main reason for me to become a leader in my clays game?**

   a. To boss my squad around.

   b. To organize my team's travel schedule.

   c. To get to the top of the *leader*board

   d. To be responsible for scoring the round.

14. **Why would I need to be creative in my clays competition?**

   a. To solve problems nobody seems to be able to answer.

   b. To push myself harder with new challenges.

   c. To stay several steps ahead of the training level of my opponents.

   d. All of the above.

Skill Drill 34: Answers to the quiz

Question Number	Answer
1	c
2	b
3	a
4	d
5	b
6	c
7	d
8	b
9	b
10	d
11	d
12	d
13	c
14	d

Next up

You passed! Now go back and review the iAPPs and the COC, because your next competition depends on your resilience. In the next chapter we'll get an ending and a beginning at the same time—the book will end and you'll just be starting the most exciting part of your career with a whole new way of looking at the pathway to success.

Test-taking is often perceived as a time to panic. However, if you think of preparing for tests as little different than the way you prepare for competitions, you'll train for them and feel great about them by using your iAPPs and trusting in your abilities.

Training Tip

The COPYCAT and SNAP iAPPs work so well that it is almost a little like gaining an advantage. Treat your GPA like a gold-medal event—because it is one.

" *It never gets easier, you just get better.*

STAR UNKNOWN WRITER

35
LAUNCH YOURSELF

Write your next high-performance chapter.

> *Don't tell me how rocky the sea is,*
> *just bring the ship in.*
>
> **— LOU HOLTZ,**
> STAR FOOTBALL COACH

This is it. The book is nearly over but you are just beginning to think and act like a champion. Congratulations to you (or your parents) for buying this book and for jumping into this high-performance program with both feet.

I mean, how many athletes have a tool kit of a GO-ZONE, an operating system of vSELFIE, iGPS and iAPPs and the COC for continuous upleveling of your competitiveness? Just a few. And you are one of the few. You even have leadership nailed with your iCEO. Who else has this stuff?

In this book I've taught you the foundation of high performance. I asked you to play so many different roles from archaeology to engineer, navigator to scientist, technician to wizard and innovator to CEO.

I asked you to believe that your mind functions like a cell phone and that you can use that cell-phone metaphor to create your successful, winning, high-performance game, with an "ON" button, an operating system and multiple applications. I asked a lot of you.

Now that you've read this book, you can do what you want with it. Bend the page corners over on pages you've found useful, insert bookmarks or highlight sections in the chapters of your favorite iAPPs, underline inspiring passages or quotes, and jot down your ideas in the margins. This book is yours.

This book is the result of many years of experience. I got into the GO-ZONE when I was a 12-year-old hockey player, though my ideas for high performance were barely taking shape in my mind, and it would take another 25 years to get it right through the practice of karate and the training of Olympians in clays sports.

All of that was fun, but what is even more fun now is knowing that the program that came out of my experience—this book—is currently in your hands (and in the hands of thousands of athletes like you). Start your push for excellence now. Right now. You are way ahead of where I was at your age. Congratulations. You have zero reason to wait. Make me proud!

Use and trust the system of amateurs and pros

You, like most of my athletes at the Olympic, professional, college level, high school and recreational level, are able to turn dreams into reality. Whatever level you reach for in your sport or in school or life, I encourage you to use and trust this system I've presented to you. It works, but only when you do.

From what my athletes have achieved and still are achieving, I believe there is no system that even comes close to giving you the advantage in your sport as this one. Your GO-ZONE alone will ensure that you stand head and shoulders above your peers. And it is your GO-ZONE, not mine, not anyone else's. Very few of your competitors will ever understand the GO-ZONE as well as you now do. Live it in everything you do.

Everything you have learned here should be new and exciting, from the overriding metaphor that your high-performance is similar to how your cell phone works, with an operating system (vSELFIE, iGPS and iAPPs) to the nitty gritty applications.

By this time (or very soon), all of your iAPPs should be at your fingertips so that you can tackle any problem in your game that comes up. Practice makes perfect and perfect practice embeds them into your subconscious mind. In this sense, you likely know more about using high-performance operating systems and applications than many top athletes. You are leading yourself to be a winner.

If there is one main theme that I want you to hold onto, it is about leadership of yourself and others:

- When you are in your **GO-ZONE**, you are standing out and acting like a leader.
- When you use **COPYCAT** and copy the skills of champions in order to fix stuff and get on the *leader*board and win, you are being a leader.

- When you use **SNAP** or any other iAPP to resolve a problem and get back on track, you are acting like a leader.
- And, especially when you use **WIZ**, you are really being a leader, as that is where you step back and clearly see what a leader like you must do to lead in every relationship.

Leading yourself to stay in your GO-ZONE is your current mission, through this program. But, be prepared. Once you use these tools to change up your game and start to perform well, everyone will look to you as a leader. And that is where sport, school and life gets really interesting and exciting, as the world of opportunity opens up for you.

Because of whom I work with, I know that the type of person who buys and reads this book is destined to be a leader. Leadership is in your future. Embrace it and go out and win. You might hurt some feelings, and some might say you are showing off, but you and I both know that you'll be showing everyone:

How to train.
How to be resilient when you lose.
How to win.
How to make friends.
How to get a better GPA.
And, how to lead.

Now, all you have to do is run with the system, use your iAPPs and do it.

Skill Drill 35: Be a high-performance leader in everything

This last Skill Drill is not as much a Skill Drill as it is a challenge. I want you to take full leadership of yourself, your clays team, your schooling, your iCEO team and all other parts of your life.

Everything.

With what you have learned in this book, and what you have already experienced, I think you already know that you are one of the few to have super skills. There is nothing you can't do to improve your game, your grades and life.

You now understand that your mind is similar to the functioning of a cell phone, or should I say, that your cell phone is similar to the functioning of your mind.

You have a basic operating system and a whole lot of terrific and

powerfully useful iAPPs. Use them. Use and demonstrate this powerful tool called your mind—to your teammates, competitors, fellow students and the parents. Demonstrate the tools you have learned in this book.

You needn't tell anyone what you are doing, as you can be the quiet leader. But nonetheless, be a leader. Your journey will start with hard work, where you might find yourself training alone at times. But trust me that that is only the first phase. Eventually, others notice and want to be a part of your journey.

So, you want to be a champion? I'm cheering you on!

Next step

This book is coming to a close, but your high-performance game is only just starting. The next step, well—that is up to you as you'll be the one writing it. You'll drive your vision with your dedication, sportsmanship, commitment and passion, along with your relationships with your team of parents, coaches, teammates and competitors. At this stage, it is all about you applying this program to your sport, your school work and your social life.

Everything depends on you now.

As you apply this program in your role as TECH, be a good one. You know your qualities and you now know the benefits of this program. With practice, the two come together until there is no program and no TECH, only you the high-performance athlete/ leader with a dynamic set of subconscious tools.

So—be a great one! I'm handing you the torch.

One last thing. Send me an email (bpalmer@sportexcel.ca) and let me know how this program has helped you in your sport and education. I'm always curious and happy to hear from my readers. And, if you love what you've learned, spread the word to your friends, teammates and competitors... well maybe not your competitors. Enjoy!

Training Tip

I am serious about you writing your next chapter. Although this is a metaphor for creating the kind of life you want, you can also write a real story. It is the last, last role I'll ask you to be.

Get out your pen and paper or your computer and start putting down your ideas as a story about your future, about your dreams, about what you are learning in competition.

When you write every day, before you know it, you have pages and pages of notes. And then you'll see how they fit into the story you want, where you can keep the brilliant stuff and put aside the rest. Surprise yourself. Your inner Dr. Seuss may be awakening...

"

I may win and I may lose,
but I will never be defeated.

— EMMITT SMITH
Star Football Player

"

ABOUT THE AUTHOR
Bob Palmer, BEd, BES
Founder, CEO and High-Performance Trainer,
SportExcel Inc.

Bob Palmer was a brilliant athlete for 10% of the time as a youth, was a brilliant coach for 50% of the time as an adult, and is now a brilliant high-performance trainer of athletes and coaches for fully 100% of the time in his present role.

In other words, at every stage in his life, Bob developed and improved on his model for excellence.

And now, he fully understands where you are coming from in your sport, and he knows what you need to take your game into the stratosphere.

Working with athletes in over 50 different sports over his career, and with such esteemed teams as the U.S. Army Marksmanship Unit and Canada Snowboard, his athletes and coaches from around the world have amassed Olympic gold, silver and bronze medals, a multitude of world cup medals of every color, championships such as high school, college, state and national and NCAA scholarship placements in multiple sports.

Bob has entirely changed the nature of high performance. As a professional educator, he made it understandable and interesting. As a systems person, he made it simple, dynamic and skills-based. This book literally makes fun out of hard work.

Bob wrote this book for you (and your parents and coaches) to equip you to think and act like a champion, as it takes a family and community to raise a teen athlete. He expects you to mark it up and bookmark your favorite pages.

And, as many of his athletes already do, he suggests you keep it at the ready in your kit or gym bag after you've read it, for situations that may (will) arise in your sport, school and life.

SPORTEXCEL BOOKS, COURSES AND HIGH-PERFORMANCE TRAINING SERVICES

Ignition Series—virtual 1-on-1 training:

The *Ignition Series* is 1-on-1 live, virtual training. This program mirrors this book and gives you and/or your teen athlete professional guidance through the program with all of the empowering high-performance tools for sport, school and life.

MIND vs TARGET: *ZoneQuest*

MIND vs TARGET: ZoneQuest is SportExcel's great high-performance program in a cost-effective video course format. This self-paced program mirrors this book and gives you and your teen 24/7 access for a year to more than 62 video lessons taught by Bob Palmer with bonus access to SportExcel's high-performance library filled with articles and podcasts. It is an ideal companion course for this book!

SportExcel books

Check out our other books on high-performance in paperback, eBook and audio versions for sport, work and life. You'll find them on Amazon and other major online book retailers or via our website:

MIND vs TARGET: The original book in the MIND vs TARGET Series for clays shooters

A MIND TO WIN: The version of MIND vs TARGET for athletes in all other sports

MENTE vs PLATO: The Spanish version of MIND vs TARGET for clays shooters

MIND vs SALES: High-performance leadership book for sales and business.

CONTACT

Email: bpalmer@sportexcel.ca

SportExcel clays website: www.sportexcelclays.com

SportExcel multi-sport website: www.sportexcel.ca

"

I'm a fighter. I'm a survivor,
and I'll get through anything people
can throw at me.

— JOHN DALY
<small>STAR GOLFER</small>

"

GLOSSARY AND CHAMPION'S CHECKLIST

The terms found in this checklist have been used throughout this book. They are made-up terms to make this subject more memorable and easy to understand. Use this as a quick reference and handy guide for what each term means, where it can be initially found in the book, and how and why it can be applied to your game.

TERM	DESCRIPTION	CHAPTER	WHY USE IT
GO-ZONE Own the Zone exercise Parts A & B	A specific feeling in your chest or gut or shoulders (some part of your body) that tells you that you are ready to compete. It signals that you are at your best	2, 3, 4	• To establish your green light signal and power up your system • To engage your high-performance mind and body with supercharged energy—every time you step into the stand • To engage your GO-ZONE in school and everything you do
Be an Archaeologist	Where you dig through your past competitions to "scrape away" the dirt (misses and bad moments) and find your times of solidly golden rounds with brilliantly smoked targets	2, 3	• To establish the ability to find GO-ZONE experiences

vSELFIE (Visualization SELFIE)	A tool to help you to enhance your game so that you can prevent nervousness in the future	5, 6	• To be proactive and fix your nervousness in competition and exams • To build absolute confidence • To visualize success • To plan your reaction to problems that may pop up in the future
NO-ZONE	When you fall out of the GO-ZONE. Your physiology may be down-leveled, such as with defeated posture where you are slouched, tense, disconnected, awkward and fatigued	7, 9, 10	• To understand that all the things that block you or hold you back are simply fixable NO-ZONE stuff
Bob's Five Visualization Rules	Bob's rules help you to better apply your vSELFIE so you can "see" the future and rehearse it in your mind	6	• To create resiliency • To see yourself win in tough situations • To imagine the stamina you'll need on those hot, rainy or windy days • To enjoy the pressure of shoot-offs (what pressure?)
Be a Navigator	Use an internal (mental) GPS to help you to act on game feedback, such as when you've missed a target or have had a meltdown	7	• To treat emotions as simply iGPS (feedback to be listened to), so that you can adapt quickly and are better equipped to learn and develop and win • To improve your game by debriefing each competition and fixing lost focus and a lost GO-ZONE

iGPS (Internal Guidance System)	The metaphor for your internal guidance system that keeps you on track, adapts quickly and guides you to success. It helps you to treat emotions such as anger or frustration simply as feedback to be listened to	7	• To debrief each competition • To fix lost focus or your GO-ZONE • To treat emotions simply as feedback to be listened to and acted upon • To adapt more quickly to new situations and be better equipped to learn and develop new skills and win
Be a TECH (Technician)	The metaphor where you actively use your passion, skills and the proper tools in this book to fix problems in your game	9	• To fix your high-performance game by applying the proper tools • To always be at the ready to tackle any problem, 24/7 • To learn from each problem you take on to become a better TECH
iAPP (Internal Application)	The strategy or tool that will be used to fix a problem, learn new skills or take leadership	9	• To fix various problems in order to get back to the GO-ZONE • To use subconsciously with practice • To use in combination with the other iAPPs to make high performance the gold standard
SNAP iAPP	This tool speeds up the process of forgetting your negative experiences.	10, 11, 14	• To fix the memory of missed targets • To banish anger or frustration with your game • To remove pre-competition or pre-exam nerves • To improve all parts of your performance in clays and in school

COPYCAT iAPP	This tool speeds up your ability to learn any new skill in sport and school by modeling your role models	12, 14	• To get back to your GO-ZONE by copying how experts do it • To fix your game problems by copying specific skills • To help with learning in school by modeling great teachers and students
30-MINUTE RULE (30MR)	A game rule that helps you to avoid the distractions, nervousness and the frustrating antics of your competitors. It ensures you are ready	13	• To give yourself space away from your competitors to better prepare for your competition • To create time to do your vSELFIE, SHREDDER and other pre-competition applications
STRETCH iAPP	A tool that allows you to change your perspective of anything, such as changing up how a target looks on ranges that you dislike to make it look like the targets on ranges you find exceptional	15, 16	• To make every range your favorite range • To love every target presentation • To change the difficult-to-see targets into easy-to-see-targets • To slow down the target and make it appear larger and brighter • To change hot summer days to cool spring days • To turn boring school books into interesting ones • To deal with an unexpected change in equipment

SHREDDER iAPP	A tool that allows you to reclaim the posture (physiology) of your GO-ZONE when you lose it and to be absolutely ready to perform. As well, this tool can be used to ensure you maintain your GO-ZONE posture all the time	17, 18	• To build your most powerful posture • To fix difficult aspects of your game by changing your physiology • To maintain your Zone over a long day of competition • To stay engaged and ready for your competition during delays or breaks in the action • To keep your adrenaline at the right level for your competition
Fitness	Using the program tools to ensure you achieve the kind of fitness that will help you maintain your GO-ZONE, feel strong and powerful, and have the energy needed to win	19	• To boost your mental well-being • To uplevel your stamina • To feel good and be healthy • To gain the physiological benefits of good posture, lung capacity and overall health • To boost your GO-ZONE and make it easy
WIRED iAPP	This tool uses adrenaline to stabilize your game	20, 21, 22	• To create constant high adrenaline in order to compete calmly
Be an Engineer	A metaphor that allows you to design how your competition day unfolds so that there are no surprises	22	• To be fired up and ready from when you wake up to when you end your competition • To ease off the adrenaline in between shots and during breaks • To wind down after competition and before sleep

WIZ iAPP	This tool helps you to specifically block out people distractions so that you can perform in your GO-ZONE. It also is the key tool for leadership	23, 24, 25	• To deal with people distractions at competitions, at school or in life • To perform consistently in competition in front of others • To become a leader in sport and other areas of your life • To empower others • To turn boring classes into dynamic ones!
Be an Archi-TECH	This metaphor helps you to design and redesign your game from one competition to another, for continuous improvement	26	• To ensure your game skills improve from competition to competition, season to season
CIRCLE OF COMPETI-TION (COC)	This tool is a way of creating ongoing improvements in your game, from competition to competition	26, 27	• To drive you forward in this very useful project called *winning* • To uplevel your abilities in every area of your life • To design continuous improvement into your game
Bob's Three Best Practice Strategies	Some of the tried and true training methods of high performers	28	• To challenge yourself To have more fun in training, competition and school • To have more free time to train

Be a Creator	A metaphor that encourages you to use your creativity to continually find new ways to uplevel your training program.	30	<ul><li>To constantly create new ways to practice</li><li>To figure out how to fix the gaps in your skills</li><li>To invent training games that simulate the stresses in your game</li><li>To develop games with and against other clays athletes in training situations so you can push them to be better and vice versa</li><li>To add dryland weight training to the needs of your game</li><li>To find new ways to use your iAPPS</li></ul>
iCEO iAPP	A metaphor that encourages you to be a Leader in Training. You enhance and round out the skills of your game by imagining being the CEO of your team where you are the talent, and your coaches, parents and all others are your team members	31, 32	<ul><li>To prepare you for your role as leader and iCEO of your family team</li><li>To gain insights into how your parents think and make decisions</li><li>To build relationships to ensure you stay in leadership mode</li><li>To learn to make better decisions</li><li>To learn how to manage your "Team"</li><li>To learn other important leadership roles such as marketing</li></ul>
Trust your ability	The time has come to stop trying to be perfect and to let your training speak for itself. Learn to stop thinking and trust your ability to perform subconsciously	33	<ul><li>To stop overthinking</li><li>To engage all of your skills in competition with no doubts</li><li>To remove all limitations and perform beyond your expectations</li></ul>

Test yourself Take the quiz!	Learn that everything you do is an experiment or a test and the results of every test make you stronger	34	• To measure your ability to recall basic concepts of this system • To introduce testing as a normal part of life where your answers are merely feedback • To demonstrate that correcting incorrect answers in everything you do is the normal way of learning
Launch yourself for future excellence	This metaphor indicates you have now learned to be forward thinking, tenacious and resilient in all of your pursuits	35	• To take personal responsibility for all of your goals in sport, school and life • To enjoy the take-off and the journey • To send Bob Palmer your feedback and successes

www.ingramcontent.com/pod-product-compliance
Lightning Source LLC
Chambersburg PA
CBHW070020100426
42740CB00013B/2569